19:99

KU-712-195

RESEARCH METHODS
IN
EDUCATIONAL MANAGEMENT

South East Essex College
of Arts & Technology
Carnarvon Road Southend-on-Sea Essex SS2 6LS
Tel: (01702) 220400 Fax: (01702) 432320 Minicom: (01702) 220642

C/R
SHL
(97) 371.72
JOH

University of Leicester MBA Series

The Principles of Educational Management by Tony Bush and John West-Burnham

Leadership and Strategic Management by John West-Burnham and Derek Glover

Managing the Curriculum by Mark Lofthouse and John West-Burnham

The Management of Professional and Support Staff by John O'Neill, David Middlewood and Derek Glover

Managing Finance and External Relations by Marianne Coleman, Tony Bush and Derek Glover

Research methods
in
educational management

by

Daphne Johnson

LONGMAN

Educational Management Development Unit
University of Leicester

RESEARCH METHODS IN EDUCATIONAL MANAGEMENT

Published by Longman Information and Reference, Longman Group UK Ltd, 6th floor, Westgate House, The High, Harlow, Essex CM20 1YR, England and Associated Companies throughout the world.

© Longman Group UK Ltd 1994

A catalogue record for this book is available from The British Library

ISBN 0-582-25136-2

Printed and bound by Athenaeum Press, Gateshead

Contents

Foreword

Research Methods in Educational Management is a key component of the course materials for the MBA in Educational Management by Distance Learning of the University of Leicester. The other texts in the series are:

The Principles of Educational Management
Leadership and Strategic Management
Managing the Curriculum
The Management of Staff
Managing Finance and External Relations

Each of these titles is an authoritative and up-to-date discussion of the central concerns of educational management. Individually the titles provide a detailed and comprehensive discussion of the topic for the student of educational management, the interested professional or the lay reader. Taken together they represent a systematic examination of the management of schools and colleges combining academic rigour and professional relevance.

These materials can be used for individual or group study and are designed to be directly applicable to personal and organisational development. The six titles in the series are written in such a way as to enhance knowledge and understanding, encourage reflection and review and support strategies for improvement.

Further information on the degree and the Educational Management Development Unit are included at the end of this volume.

Tony Bush
Professor of Educational Management

John West-Burnham
Lecturer in Educational Management

Series Editors

This text has been prepared by Daphne Johnson for the Educational Management Development Unit (EMDU), University of Leicester. Part II includes edited versions of texts relating to research methods relevant to educational management.

Daphne Johnson draws on her own extensive experience as a researcher and her many years of post-graduate teaching of research methods in the Department of Government, Brunel University. Dr Johnson now works as an academic consultant in the field of educational management and research methods.

Preface

You may have studied research methods before, or perhaps this is your first encounter with the subject. In either case, I hope my text will provide the grounding you need for the successful design and completion of your own research project.

From time to time, as you read Chapters 1 and 2, I shall ask you to undertake an *Activity*, the term used here for thinking which makes a bridge between what I and other professional researchers have written, and your own situation as a student preparing for a project.

At the end of Part I, together with a full set of references, I include a short list of recommended reading, which will help you to follow up particular aspects of research in more detail. Part II contains the Readings to which you are particularly directed in Part I.

This book has been designed for students in the Educational Management Development Unit (EMDU), University of Leicester. It will also be useful for other students of educational management who embark on a research project as part of their course of study.

The ethos of research into educational management is to assist the development of effective school and college management. Your research-based project enquiry is meant to lead to professional reflection and, where appropriate, a commitment to change. The hope is that all concerned with your enquiry will be helped by it.

Daphne Johnson

Acknowledgements

The publishers are indebted to the following for permission to reproduce extracts from:

Blalock, H. (1970) *An Introduction to Social Research*, New Jersey: Prentice-Hall Inc.; Hoinville R., Jowell, R. et al. (1978) *Survey Research Practice*, Heinemann; Kogan, M., Johnson, D., Packwood, T. and Whitaker, T. (1984) *School Governing Bodies*, Heinemann; Scott, J. (1990) *A Matter of Record*, Cambridge Polity Press; Cohen, L. and Manion, L. (1980) *Research Methods in Education*, Croom Helm; Kane, E. (1985) *Doing Your Own Research*, Marion Boyars; Johnson, D., and Ransom, E. (1983) *Family and School*, Croom Helm; Powney, J. and Watts, M. (1987) *Interviewing in Educational Research*, Routledge and Kegan Paul; the *Cambridge Journal of Education*. (1987) 17, 2, 'The primary school staff relationships project: origins, aims and methods' by Jennifer Nias; 'The experience of fieldwork; or insider dealings, who profits?' by Geoff Southworth; 'Checking and adjusting the lens: case study clearance' by Robin Yeomans; Hilsum, S. and Kane, B.S. (1971) *The Teacher's Day*, NFER; Johnson, D. (1984) 'Planning small-scale research' in Bell, S. et. al. (Eds) *Conducting Small-Scale Investigations in Educational Management*, Harper and Row; Haywood, P. and Wragg, E.C. (1978) *Evaluating the Literature*, School of Education, Nottingham University; M. T. Lofthouse, and T. Whiteside *The Literature Review II*.

Part I

1 Thinking about research

This chapter asks you to give some general thought to research issues, before going on (in Chapters 2 and 3) to look at some 'best practice' research methods, and the research tools which can be used. Advice on tackling your own project is given in Chapter 4.

1.1 What is research?

As part of your course, you are going to undertake a research-based project. 'Research' is a word which is often loosely used. I offer the following as a working definition which you may like to come back to when you begin to make your own project plans. I define research as:

> *a focused and systematic enquiry that goes beyond generally available knowledge to acquire specialised and detailed information, providing a basis for analysis and elucidatory comment on the topic of enquiry.*

My definition may lack sparkle and brevity, but it contains a number of key words and phrases which students undertaking research-based projects need to grapple with:

Focused
Research always focuses on a specific topic, not a broad field of interest. 'Educational management' is not a suitable focus for research enquiry. Research would need to home in on a particular aspect of educational management, such as for example 'the governance of grant-maintained schools' or 'structures for the accreditation of prior learning'.

Systematic
Research is not a 'catch-as-catch-can' enterprise. Although many research approaches rely on imaginative design and may follow intuitive paths, the approach must have structure and system.

Beyond (generally available knowledge)
Research is not a question of collating available information into a telephone-directory type format. Some of the data on which research relies may be

available only to a restricted audience, or are perhaps under the control of particular individuals. Research may take an analytic approach to information already in the public domain, or combine it with less readily available data in order, in the classic phrase, to 'push back the frontiers of knowledge' on the research topic.

A basis for analysis and elucidatory comment

This rather ponderous phrase from my definition of research embraces some important characteristics. Data acquired must provide a basis for what researchers conclude from their enquiries. Research conclusions do not (or should not) derive from preconceptions or received wisdom about a subject. The findings of the research may overturn preconceptions and challenge received wisdom, or they may confirm either or both. But it is what the research enquiry discovers that must be subjected to analysis by the researcher, whose task it then is to offer 'elucidatory comment' or exposition which will help other interested parties to think freshly about the subject.

Activity 1.1

Candidates for *Mastermind* or other knowledge-based quiz shows may claim to have undertaken 'research' into their chosen subject. Does their use of the word match my definition?

My comment

Quiz-show type research may be specialised and detailed but it cannot, by definition, go beyond generally available knowledge or there would be no possibility of establishing the 'right' or 'wrong' answer to questions posed. Also, however impressed we may be by the in-depth familiarity of contestants with their subject (and their capacity for instant recall while under stress!) we learn nothing new about their topic. Analysis and explanation are not called for from contestants, only facts.

1.2 Some first-base problems of social research

In my experience, research into educational management comes under the heading of social rather than scientific research. 'Scientific management' is still an evocative phrase, but it is not a central feature of management courses today. The prime resource of management is people, and where people and their behaviour, their forms of organisation and their associations are the subject of enquiry, we are into the field of social research.

Accordingly, and even at this early stage, we must give some thought to 'first-base' problems of social research which may otherwise take us by surprise later on.

If the subject of our research is to be people and the ways they are inter-linked by management processes, we must recognise certain ethical implications of our work.

It may

> *bring disturbance to the working arrangements, the lifestyle or the relationships of the people we involve.* To be the subject of research is not a neutral experience. The simplest questionnaire may cause those who complete it to think in a new way about some aspect of their life or work which they had previously taken for granted, and a penetrating interview may uncover satisfactions or resentments individuals never knew they had. Even to be required to clarify in what areas you have management responsibilities, or where you count yourself as being subject to management by others, can be a disturbing experience.

Research may also

> *seek confidential information.* Confidentiality is a prime ethical issue which researchers must face from the outset. If information is imparted in confidence, how should it be handled as research data?

Another ethical issue confronting the researcher is the question of

> *the motives of researcher and researched.* Is the researcher making the enquiry for professional and potentially developmental reasons, or out of idle curiosity, or to meet the requirements of higher degree examiners? Is the research participant collaborating in the enquiry for professional or personal reasons? Have they an 'axe to grind', which may cause them to see the research as a sharpening stone?

In Chapter 4 I offer more detailed advice on how these ethical issues should be handled in research. For now I just want to alert you to them, but there is one broad principle to stress.

> *The ethos of research into educational management is to assist the development of effective school and college management. Your research-based project enquiry is meant to lead to professional reflection and, where appropriate, a commitment to change. Your motives in undertaking it, and the motives of those who collaborate with you, will no doubt be mixed, but the hope is that all concerned with your enquiry will be helped and not hindered by it.*

This should certainly be your aim, and if your research is carried out in your own institution it is likely that you will be able to make some recommendations for helpful change. To this extent your project might be seen as 'action research'. However, in the research world the term 'action research' has a particular technical meaning, which I briefly discuss at the end of Chapter 2.

1.3 How much do you need to know about research, before embarking on a research-based project?

Although your research will probably be single-handed and small-scale, you are in effect joining the research community by undertaking a project of the kind required. It is important that you are aware of what is deemed 'good practice' in professional research, and have some understanding of the principles which underlie good practice.

You also need to have some familiarity with a range of tried and tested methods of social research, and the areas of enquiry for which they are suited. Chapters 2 and 3 aim to provide this familiarisation, and Chapter 4 will address the particular situation of the single-handed project researcher. In the remaining paragraphs of this introductory chapter I will try to deal briefly with the principles and practice of 'good' research.

❑ Schools of thought in research

There are generally perceived to be two main areas of preference in the social research community: those who favour quantitative studies and those who value qualitative work. Quantitative research is interested in aggregating data, most of which are assigned numerical values. It relies on certain accepted categorisations, which enable the making of generalised statements. For example, the annual report on Social Trends by the Government Statistical Service (GSS), from its quantitative enquiries, may include a statement about the number of school pupils attending independent schools (GSS 1992, Table 3.5).

Qualitative research, on the other hand, is interested in the complexities of human decision-making and behaviour, and may, for example, seek to discover what sets of circumstances lead particular families to use the independent sector for their children's education (Johnson, 1987).

It should not be assumed that large-scale and small-scale research are synonymous with the quantitative and qualitative schools of research, nor indeed that research cannot span both modes of enquiry.

In the past, researchers have perceived two distinct 'schools of thought', sometimes referred to as 'positivism' and 'relativism' underlying the quantitative and the qualitative approaches to research. This book does not have space to tackle the philosophy of research in any depth. It must suffice to say that quantitative (or 'positivist') research followed the scientific mode, aiming at objectivity, standard procedures and replicability. Qualitative (or 'relativist') research, on the other hand, took the view that all human life is experienced and indeed constructed from a subjective point of view, and that social research should seek to elicit the 'meaning' of events and phenomena from the point of view of participants.

While these two approaches do have different philosophical bases, a growing body of social research takes a stand somewhere between the two schools of thought. It is recognised that no piece of social research can be entirely objective, since no researcher is value free. Even in an overtly rigorous, quantitative, head-counting study, some implicit decisions have already been made as to which heads are worth counting. (In scientific research too, there has been a move towards acknowledging that absolute replicability of experiments is scarcely possible, since many potential variables may intrude from outside the researcher's frame of reference (Popper, 1979).

In qualitative research too, experience has shown that although all data are coloured by the meaning which the data provider attaches to them — a meaning which may not be fully shared by the researcher — such data are nevertheless the rational outcome of the way the research participant sees the world. Although we may not always know in full depth what a participant *means*, we have to go by what they *say*, and make the most sensitive interpretation we can of it, from the basis of our own world view.

(If you do not have a social science background, but are interested to follow up some of these briefly expressed ideas, Bryman, 1988, focuses on the quantitative/qualitative debate. Another relevant text is Berger and Luckman, 1967).

Reputable social research will always give at least a nod in the direction of the scientific model, by attempting to clarify and justify its own structure and scope. Although complete replication of a social enquiry may never be possible, as some circumstances will always have changed, the researcher should do all that is possible to enable replication, by exposing the decisions which underlie choice of area, institution and respondents, giving details of the research tools used, and explaining the forms of categorisation relied on, and what their weaknesses are. (For example, some forms of social class categorisation have an almost entirely male frame of reference, and have very limited use in categorising women).

Because the meaning of events is always subjectively perceived, researchers should try to provide circumstances in which participants are as free as possible to communicate their own view of the world, and are not unduly influenced by the preconceptions of the researcher. Leading questions, which admit of only one 'respectable' answer must be avoided, and participants should be acknowledged as valuable contributors to the research in their own right, a situation which should minimise 'interviewer-pleasing'.

❏ Triangulation

Another way in which social research can be strengthened is by 'triangulation', that is, by homing in on research evidence from several points of view. If you rely on a single source of evidence, there is the possibility that some inaccuracies or prejudices incorporated in that evidence may be slipping by you. If on the other hand different sources of evidence lead to a broadly similar picture, you can have more confidence in your conclusions. For example, when accrediting National Records of Achievement at a school or college, external assessors are always interested to hear an account of the process by which the records are prepared and checked, as described by the Records of Achievement coordinator. But they also want to examine the Records themselves, and discuss with students and tutorial staff their 'grass roots' experience of the Records of Achievement programme. This is a form of 'technique triangulation' which is equally applicable to internal research.

As Hammersley and Atkinson (1989, p.199) point out, 'what is involved in triangulation is not the combination of different kinds of data *per se*, but rather an attempt to relate different sorts of data in such a way as to counteract various possible threats to the validity of our analysis'.

I have written elsewhere (Johnson, 1984) about the relevance of some of these issues for the single-handed researcher, and later I shall ask you to read parts of my article which are reproduced in Part II. For now, my intention is only to help you become aware of some of the limitations of social research, which will inevitably also limit the validity of your own research-based enquiry into educational management.

Now I turn to the specific question of 'insider' research, which is what your project is most likely to be.

1.4 What are the strengths and weaknesses of doing research in your own institution?

If you work in a school or college, educational management is going on around you, throughout the working day. If you do not work in a school or college, your research situation is more directly discussed in Chapter 4. You may nevertheless find it useful to read on about the advantages and disadvantages of 'insider' research.

The obvious place to look for a particular aspect of management which can be the focus of your project is within your own institution. If you decide to do this, certain advantages will be immediately apparent:

1. Some of the management issues in your institution which would justify close study are probably already known to you.

2. These issues are 'on your doorstep', and may not require you to travel to new sites either during or outside working hours.

3. You already have a colleague relationship with some of the people involved in these management issues, whether they are on the receiving end of hierarchical management edicts, drawn into decision-making on a collegial basis, or fulfilling an unequivocally executive role.

These are real advantages, but they do not mean that undertaking research in your own institution will be entirely without problems.

To begin with, you must reject the idea that

(a) 'nobody will mind if I do some research where I work'

or the other equally mistaken idea that

(b) nobody will notice if I do some research where I work'

Later I address the question of covert research, which is the research method implied in (b). For the single-handed project student it is definitely not a good method, nor is it really feasible, as I explain below. But first, let us look at the idea expressed in (a) that explicit permission to undertake research in your own institution is not required. Quite wrong!

❏ Access for research

All researchers *must* negotiate research access to their field of enquiry. You will be asking other people to contribute their time and knowledge to your enquiry, and this must be agreed with them as a favour, not assumed to be your right. Even if all the people you approach as research participants are in less senior positions than yourself, their agreement to participate must be explicitly asked for. And in the unlikely event that your single-handed research will be confined to school or college archives, and will involve no questioning or observation of colleagues, you must still bear in mind that the care of these archives is someone's responsibility, and their permission is needed before you make use of them.

The negotiation of research access, if appropriately carried through, can make all the difference to the success of a project. It is more fully discussed in Chapter 4. I turn now to some of the implications of insider research for the researcher's role.

The first thing to recognise is that in your own institution you already have an accustomed role. You probably have a job description, and you certainly operate within a set of expectations from students and from other workers at the school or college as to the part you are there to play. When you undertake research you are taking on a new role of detached enquirer, and this is additional to and to some degree separated from your usual work. Both you and your colleagues need to be clear about this, otherwise you may find yourself missing research opportunities, or your colleagues may become confused by changes in your working style and conversation.

If your research is to include interviewing in your own school or college — and the opportunity to arrange this without undue difficulty or loss of time can be a real point in favour of insider research — then the interview will clearly place you in a new role *vis-à-vis* the person interviewed. This person may be senior to you in the institution, but in the interview situation you are the controlling party. In all cases remember that your working relationships will continue when the research relationship has been concluded. Tact will be needed to ensure that the penetration and relative objectivity of your enquiries does not cast a long-term blight on your day-to-day interaction with your colleagues.

❏ Other preliminaries to research

The points I have made so far about insider research relate mainly to yourself and your continuing role in the school or college. So far as the research itself is concerned, hazards to look out for are a possible failure to focus your research on a clear-cut topic, and the increased possibility that preconceptions rather than research findings will dominate your analysis.

Familiarity with the complex inter-relationships between individuals, groups and departments in an institution sometimes makes it difficult to 'see the wood for the trees'. Researching in your own school or college, you must take extra care to identify the particular management issue which is your subject of study, otherwise your research may stray endlessly on, continually uncovering new complexities of possible cause and effect.

Equally, and especially if you feel you already know the answer to a problem situation which your research is to explore, you should guard against making your envisaged solution the frame of reference for all your enquiries. Systematic research, a quality included in my definition at the beginning of this section, explores its subject in an even-handed way, and does not rule out the possibility of genuine enlightenment along the way.

Before going on to Chapter 2, which gets down to detail about research methods, take a few moments to mull over the points I have made so far. Then apply them to your own experience, as stated in Activity 1.2.

Activity 1.2

Have you ever been asked to take part in someone else's research? This may have been an encounter with a market researcher in a shopping precinct or at home, a request to help with school-required project enquiries by pupils, or an approach at work from a colleague or a member of an organisation with which your institution is linked (for example a local education authority, diocesan board, or FEFC).

cont'd...

...cont'd

It will help to clarify your own expectations about desirable standards for research if you try to answer the following questions:

- If you agreed to assist with someone else's research, why did you do so?

- If you refused, why was this?

- If you took part, what satisfaction did you derive from this?

- Did anything about the research encounter annoy or dissatisfy you?

- Did you ever hear anything more about the research in which you took part?

My comment

Obviously I cannot know what your answers to these questions are. But answering them may have reminded you of some of the points I have been making in this chapter.

Research is not a haphazard or slapdash activity. It has to be systematic, and give assurance to those taking part, as well as to those using its findings, that it has been properly planned.

However well designed, research makes demands on the time and energy of those who cooperate with it. Their important contribution to the research must be acknowledged, and if possible rewarded by making sure that they hear about the eventual outcomes of the research in which they have participated. In Chapter 4, I shall return to the question of feedback about research to those who contribute to it.

2 Research approaches

In this chapter I want to take you on a brief conducted tour of the main ways in which research can be tackled. We will look at surveys, case studies, documentary research, the experimental approach and non-reactive research. Taken separately, not all of these approaches are equally suitable for single-handed project research, but they are all classic methods on which professional researchers have based their findings. Your own research design will need to take account of them, and is likely to use some combination of these research approaches.

2.1 The survey approach

A small-scale survey may well form part of your project. You will also almost certainly be reading about published survey work, as part of your literature review. Working through the principles of survey research which I cover in this section will help you to make an assessment of the quality of the surveys you read about.

❑ Definition

Surveys have been in common use throughout the twentieth century. A simple definition which covers all types of survey activity is:

eliciting equivalent information from an identified population

Key words in my definition help us to look at the survey activity in more detail:

Information

The kind of information sought by a survey may be straightforward 'facts', attitudes or opinions at the time of the survey approach. Surveys are not a reliable guide to the future. As Hoinville and Jowell (1978) point out, they should 'be regarded essentially as a means by which we can document, analyse and interpret past and present attitudes and behaviour patterns. By exposing trends they will certainly provide clues about the future, but they are only clues.' (p.184).

Equivalent information

The purpose of a survey is to give a research basis for collated description or comparison. Accordingly, the same *kind* of information is sought from all respondents. This need influences the way the information is obtained.

Eliciting equivalent information

'Eliciting' implies something more proactive than just 'collecting' information. The respondent has to be prompted by specific questions to make relevant statements of fact or opinion. Because *equivalent* information is needed, the survey questions are standardised. They may be posed in a face-to-face or telephone interview, or through a self-completion questionnaire.

Activity 2.1

A survey in the field of education management might, for example, enquire from INSET organisers at a given body of schools what arrangements or opportunities have been provided for appraisal training/preparation of teaching staff at the school, during a given period.

If you were carrying out such an appraisal training survey, what kinds of 'equivalent information' would you want to obtain?

My comment

The easy answer to that question is that it depends what kind of report you want to write! Remember that your findings must be based on the information you acquire, not on any preconceptions you may have about the topic. Since my suggestion was of a survey approach to INSET *organisers*, you would presumably be seeking factual information about arrangements already carried out, or arrangements formally planned for appraisal training — workshops, seminars etc. Your questions would need to stress *formally* planned, for future events. Hopeful expectations, or vaguely formulated plans, would not be useful for your survey.

Another key phrase in my definition of survey activity is:

Identified population

The people approached in a survey are known as the 'population'. They are the desired providers of the information sought, and are sometimes referred to as 'units of enquiry'. A *census* is a survey which approaches an *entire* identified population — *all* the headteachers of secondary schools in England and Wales, for example, or *all* the persons resident in Great Britain on a given night in April. (The latter example is the population covered by the decennial Census, last carried out by the Office of Population Censuses and Surveys in 1991. An article in *Social Trends 21* (GSS 1991, p.13) outlines the plans which were made for the content of that Census. *Social Trends 22* (GSS 1992, p.233) gives details of some other major government surveys regularly drawn on for this annual publication).

Sampling

Most survey designs identify a population (such as all secondary headteachers) and then approach a *sample* of them. Sampling is a research methods issue which cannot be adequately dealt with here. *Part II* contains an extract from Blalock (1970) about probability sampling. It is an American text, but the principles it explains are common to all survey enquiry. As you read, bear in mind that if statistical analysis is to be applied to research findings, ideally the research should be based on a probability sample.

◎ Reading 1

READ Blalock (1970) p.97 next, then return to this text.

My comment

For the single-handed researcher, the main point to note from Blalock's discussion of probability is that any sample is likely to be biased in some way. Researchers who design probability samples do so in order to minimise bias, and increase the likelihood that findings from their research can reasonably be generalised to a wider population.

The extract from Blalock which you have just read is the nearest we shall get to statistical theory in this book. (Useful more specialist books on this subject are Anderson and Zelditch, 1975; Blalock, 1972 or, for a brief introduction to the principles involved in statistical analysis, Kalton, 1966. A more recent text which gives some space to statistical principles is de Vaus, 1992).

❏ Non-probability sampling

Surveys lose their valuable quality of providing 'generalisable' information if probability sampling is not employed. However, non-probability samples, sometimes called 'judgement' samples are frequently used in small scale surveys, and also in market research. Quota sampling is the most common form of judgement sample. Hoinville and Jowell (1978, p.87) explain how this is done:

> Interviewers are supplied with 'quotas' or set specifications regarding the number of people of various kinds that they must interview. Provided that the specification is fulfilled, they are free to interview whom they wish within the designated area.

> The idea behind quota sampling is that much of the variability in human behaviour is accounted for if the sample is made properly representative in respect of the 'quota' variables — usually sex, age and social class. It is argued that the quota controls, which are in effect a stratifying procedure, reduce variability and that any bias that may arise in the selection of individuals within the quota groups is unlikely to be serious, provided that the interviewer operates intelligently and with an understanding of what is required.

This 'quota' principle, of trying to ensure that your sample spans the main characteristics of the population being surveyed, may be more feasible than probability sampling for single-handed researchers doing small-scale surveys.

Activity 2.2

If you were an advisory teacher, asked to carry out an appraisal training survey of the kind mentioned in Activity 2.1 (p.14), what population of schools would you aim to approach? Would you undertake a census of all INSET organisers, or try to select a sample?

My comment

Scope of coverage is one of the first things which has to be decided in survey research. Did you differentiate between primary and secondary schools when deciding on your population? Appraisal training is applicable to both the primary and secondary sectors, so a survey could cover both, but an advisory teacher working single-handedly might prefer to focus on one sector only. Even so, the number of schools surveyed would need to be small, and these might be linked by area or perhaps to a cluster grouping. If so, it would be reasonable to attempt a *census* of all INSET organisers, rather than trying to select a sample.

I took the example of an advisory teacher as such a teacher could well have access to several schools. A teacher interested in appraisal training but who had access to only *one* school, might do better to take a different research approach. In a large school they might survey teachers at different levels of seniority who had undergone appraisal training. In a small school, rather than seek 'equivalent' information through a survey, a researcher could make a case study of appraisal training from the point of view of appraisers and appraisees.

❑ Need for a common frame of reference between survey research designer and the population researched

This is a point often overlooked in the research literature on surveys. Because the survey approach is standardised, there is little opportunity to explore subtleties of meaning. Some broadly common frame of reference between researcher and researched must be assumed. If it is lacking, the survey approach could be unproductive. (It might, for example, be difficult for the British Medical Association to glean helpful information from practitioners of alternative medicine by means of a survey, because of fundamental differences of vocabulary and approach).

Although a student studying education management will have much in common with educational professionals, there could be some problems of shared meaning in any survey approach to parents, pupils, governors or support staff at a school. Cultural and generational differences in the use of language can be subtle but important, and will mean that particular care (and some pilot trials) must be given to the design of the research instrument.

❑ What are the strengths of the survey approach?

There are several good reasons for the popularity of the survey research method.

Breadth of coverage

Because the research tool is standardised, once the questionnaire or interview schedule has been designed it is usually possible to approach a relatively large number of respondents.

Generalisability/comparability

Survey findings can be generalised to a wider population, if probability sampling has been employed. If comparable definitions of basic variables have been used, it is also possible to compare results with those of other surveys. (Stacey, 1969, discusses the definition of basic variables such as education, household and income).

Descriptive power

Surveys typically produce a large amount of factual information which can be cross-tabulated in many ways to provide a wealth of description. This can give a basis for further research with a more explanatory aim. Moser and Kalton (1985, p.4) suggest that surveys should be seen as 'one way, and a supremely useful one, of exploring the field, of collecting data *around* as well as directly *on* the subject of study, so that the problem is brought into focus and the points worth pursuing are suggested'.

❏ Weaknesses of the survey approach

Shallow coverage

Because of the standardised approach, surveys do not give the opportunity to explore a topic in depth. Questions asked must be unequivocal in meaning, and responses must be fitted into a limited range.

Unsuitable for 'sensitive' issues

Respondents may need encouragement and a sense of rapport with the researcher and the research, if they are to provide factual information or opinion on 'sensitive' issues. Survey interviews or questionnaires do not have the flexibility to enable this kind of supportive atmosphere. (In a period of continuing educational change, some teachers would contend that all aspects of educational management are 'sensitive' issues!)

Scope for bias

If the sample is flawed in some way (i.e. it is not in fact representative of the 'identified population') then generalising from the survey findings can produce seriously biased statements.

◎ Reading 2

*Turn now to **Part II**, and read the extract from Hoinville and Jowell (1978) p.103, about possible errors of interpretation in surveys. It sums up some of my points about the limitations of the survey approach. Then return to this text.*

❏ Examples of survey work in educational management

Much of what I have said so far about the survey approach applies mainly to large-scale surveys. It is important to realise what such surveys can achieve. In earlier times, the Central Advisory Council for Education prepared reports for the (then) Ministry of Education, based on high quality and extensive survey work. One such was the *Crowther Report '15 to 18'* published by HMSO in two volumes in 1959. If you are interested to see a good example of large scale survey work in the field of education you could take a look at this report, especially Volume II, which gives the survey designs.

Of recent years there have been few large-scale nationally-funded education surveys, but various funding bodies have commissioned or supported research focused on particular aspects of education or educational management, several of which have used a survey approach. For example, an investigation of where the balance should lie between parental choice and LEA management was carried out by NFER (Stillman, 1986; Stillman and Maychell, 1986). Two questionnaire surveys were made, of 125 education authorities and divisions, and of 3,000 families whose children had transferred to or were about to transfer to secondary school in one of four authorities. More recently, the Leverhulme Trust funded an enquiry into grant-maintained schools (Bush, et al. 1993), which on the smaller scale appropriate to the limited field of enquiry made a questionnaire survey of all grant-maintained schools in operation by September 1991 (100 schools). Any of these works is worth consulting to see what surveys on this scale can achieve.

❏ Resources needed for survey research

For interview surveys, *time* must be available for short-term but intensive involvement in the field by researchers.

If questionnaires are used, *funds* are needed for postal delivery, unless there is access to some other means of effective distribution. The whole point of collecting equivalent information through a survey is to find out the distribution of replies to a given question.

Some *means of collating* the information acquired must therefore be set up. In presenting collated information from a small-scale survey, care must however be taken not to mislead as to the scale of the findings. If only a small number of people have been surveyed, findings should not be reported in percentage terms. For example, if you have surveyed 30 parents, 20 of whom say they attended the school's Open Evening while 10 did not, the statement that '66 per cent' attended gives a false impression of scale. Better to say that 'two-thirds of parents surveyed attended the Open Evening'.

It is unlikely that your research will be on a scale to justify computerised analysis, but should this be necessary several software packages exist for the analysis of social survey data, notably SPSS (Nie, 1975).

Single-handed researchers do not typically use a survey as their *only* approach to a field of enquiry. They are more likely to use interviews and questionnaires as part of a more rounded case study, the form of research to which we now turn.

2.2 Case study approach

Although surveys are the form of research most familiar to the general public, case studies have in recent years been regularly used by professional researchers. They are normally local to a particular area and concentrated in their coverage. Case studies are labour-intensive, but they call on the labour of the researcher(s) already employed on the project. Unlike some other forms of research approach, case studies are particularly suitable for single-handed project researchers. You should therefore give special attention to this section, with its associated reading, and return to it when you are planning your own research design.

❏ Definition

> *A case study is an enquiry which uses multiple sources of evidence. It investigates a contemporary phenomenon within its real-life context, when the boundaries between phenomenon and context are not clearly evident.*

This definition is based on that of Yin (1984). Again we need to 'unpack' the key elements of the definition.

Multiple sources of evidence
Case study is a research *approach*. Several research *tools* may be used to accumulate data, for example interviewing (see Chapter 3, Section 3.2), observation (Chapter 3, Section 3.3), and use of records (Chapter 3 Section 3.4).

Investigates a contemporary phenomenon
Case studies are concerned with the interaction of factors and events over a period of time. Usually the study is of a phenomenon still in evidence at the present day, though not necessarily new or recent. Case study should not be confused with case work (in the fields of psychology, psychiatry or social

work). Issues, rather than the situations of individuals, are the focus of case study in educational management or other forms of social research.

Investigates a phenomenon within its real life context

The case study is a naturalistic type of enquiry (Denzin, 1978). It involves the systematic gathering of evidence but does not require an experimental situation.

The boundaries between phenomenon and context are not clearly evident

Common sense perceived boundaries to case studies are not ring fences. As the study progresses, the boundaries appear increasingly permeable. But where a social phenomenon has an institutional form (e.g. a school governing body) there is a more immediate sense of structure than for a more exploratory enquiry (e.g. the development and launch of a new marketing policy for a college).

Activity 2.3

Remember that a case study uses 'multiple sources of evidence'. If you envisaged making a case study of the functions and operations of a particular school or college governing body, what kinds of evidence would you try to obtain, and from what sources? Spend a few minutes making rough plans and writing them down.

My comment

In the early 1980s I helped to design and carry out a number of case studies of school governing bodies. You might like to compare your initial ideas, with this example of the case study approach.

◎ Reading 3

*Turn to **Part II**, p.106, and read the passage from Kogan et al. (1984) which describes our research methods for the School Governing Bodies project. The account given of our methods is unusually full, and includes passing reference to some of the* *issues referred to elsewhere in this text, such as triangulation, and the negotiation of access. Some of our efforts went into ensuring that all members of the research team were kept fully informed of the field work by other members, and that all analysis was jointly discussed. A single-handed researcher would not of course have the opportunity for this kind of cross-checking. As you read, make a note of the different sources of evidence and the research tools we used. Then return to this text.*

I hope the reading from Kogan (1984) has served to exemplify Yin's definition of case study. We now continue with a formal analysis of the advantages and limitations of case study research, still using the governing body work as an example.

❑ Strengths of the case study approach
Copes with complexity
The reading from Kogan (1984) covers eight case studies, all related to a single project enquiry. But even a single case study can provide descriptive data, address problems of meaning, examine the record of past events and relate it to present activity. Moreover several different 'units of enquiry' can be approached (e.g. governors, parents, teachers, community workers), and their participation enlisted by differing means.

Intelligible, non-technical findings
Because many sources of evidence are used, the picture which emerges is 'in the round', compared with the one-dimensional image provided by the average survey. Case study based reports tend to be easily readable, able to be understood by non-researchers, and hence a more widely accessible form of research outcome than is sometimes the case with other methods.

Can provide interpretations of other similar cases.
Although full generalisability cannot be claimed for case studies, they have the property of 'relatability' (Bassey, 1981). The rounded picture a case study gives is sufficiently lifelike to be compared with other examples, when similarities and differences can readily be identified.

❑ Weaknesses of the case study approach
Lack of scientific rigour
This is the chief criticism levelled at the case study approach. There is no 'book of rules' for the design of a case study. Each must depend on the nature of the phenomenon investigated, and the particular circumstances in which it occurs. In the reading from Kogan (1984) it is plain that innumerable individual judgements were made about the feasibility of particular forms of

enquiry, for example the types of in-school observation carried out, and in particular the contacts made with community groups (see final paragraph of the reading). Case studies rely heavily on the skill and industry of the individual researcher.

Possible uniqueness of the material
If a case study focuses on a unique institution or phenomenon, it may be of esoteric interest, but there is no bonus of 'relatability'. Selection of case study sites and phenomena examined is therefore crucial for the usefulness of the study for a wider audience. Non-uniqueness is the aim. In the governing body research, multiple case studies made it possible to cover a range of types of school (primary, secondary, special, voluntary-aided), but some of the secondary schools covered an age range (12–16) which is not typical of the majority of such schools, and this had its effect on the range of interests of the governing body.

Possibility of uneven access to all aspects of the phenomenon studied
Although the intention is to make a study 'in the round', the exploratory nature of the work may tempt the researcher down a particular pathway, to the detriment of other lines of enquiry. Being 'led by the data' (Yin, 1984) can result in an untidy bundle of findings, rather than a rounded picture.

❑ Can the case study stand alone? Its place in a research framework
The purpose of research by case study is not merely to portray a specific situation, but to do so in a way that illuminates some more general principle (Nisbet and Watt, 1984). The rounded picture which the good case study provides is not sufficient in itself. Some conceptual analysis must be made of the elements which make up the picture. This analysis can then either be used to create a grounded theory (Glaser and Strauss, 1967), or be related to some existing body or bodies of knowledge.

The creation of grounded theory is the line taken by many case study researchers who use their specialised data to illuminate a more general principle. 'Grounded' theory is theory based on emerging data, rather than on an advance hypothesis. Throughout the fieldwork, the researcher searches for the major themes that can be used to organise the data. (See, for example, the concluding chapter of Woods (1979), in which the writer discusses the conceptual themes which have emerged from his study of *The Divided School*).

Another way of analysing the findings of a case study is to relate them to some existing body or bodies of knowledge. In the Kogan study of school governing bodies, findings were discussed and explained in terms of previous studies of the political–administrative system, institutional studies and analyses of professionalism in education (Chapters 3, 4 and 5 of Kogan, 1984).

Nisbet and Watt (1984) point out that the survey and case study approaches can be used to complement each other. A survey can be followed up by case studies, to test out conclusions by examining specific instances. This combination of methods was used by Bush, et al. (1993), who followed up their survey of grant-maintained schools with case studies at five of the schools. Alternatively, Nisbet and Watt suggest, where a new problem is being opened up for research, 'the case study may precede a survey, to identify key issues' (Nisbet and Watt 1984, p.77).

The single-handed researcher may not have the resources to combine case study work with other research approaches. It is all the more important to relate the case study to existing theories, or illuminate the study by creating your own framework of concepts from the data obtained.

❑ Resources needed for the case study approach

In undertaking case study work *time* must be available for extended field work. Since several research techniques are to be used, they may overlap in time. For example, meetings might be observed or interviews undertaken during the period of awaiting the return of questionnaires. It is more likely however that research opportunities will not fit neatly into a brief period, but rather will be intermittent, and this must be allowed for in the research design.

For the case study approach, more than for other forms of research, *access to a variety of research settings* is likely to be needed. If, for example, you were to make a case study of how your school or college governing body handles curriculum issues, you might need access to main governing body meetings and governing body sub-committee meetings, to governors themselves and to certain teaching staff, to minutes of past meetings and LEA documents, and perhaps to any LEA or other governor support services whose training materials and courses have been used. (The negotiation of access is further discussed in Chapter 4).

To undertake case study work successfully, researchers must be *familiar with a range of research skills and tools*. Case study workers cannot simply be specialists in, for example, interviewing. They must also be equipped for documentary study and observation.

We move on now to consider documentary research.

2.3 Documentary research

Documentary research relies primarily on the use of available printed data as a source of evidence. In your own small scale project, your use of documents is likely to be only one of a range of research approaches. However, being aware of the principles on which documentary research is based will help you to examine critically and analytically any documents you want to use as sources of evidence in your own research.

Scott (1990) defines a document as 'any artefact which has as its central feature an inscribed text'. Such documents may provide information from the distant or more recent past. All documentary research is to some degree retrospective.

Most documentary research into management relies on printed sources and these will be the main focus of this section. Nevertheless, one can envisage documentary research into the development of management training which might be based on a study of training videos over a number of years. The same rigorous approach which I shall advocate for the study of written texts (Chapter 3, Section 3.4) would need to be applied to the analysis of videos.

Scott (1990) also puts forward a useful classification of modern documents, by authorship and access. The question of access, that is, the availability of documents to people other than their authors, is of central importance for researchers.

◎ Reading 4

*You will find Scott's (1990) typology, and his discussion of the various types of document available, in **Part II**, p.112. Read it, and then return to this text.*

Scott's analysis is helpful in widening our understanding of the many types of document in existence, and some of the restrictions which may be placed in the way of their availability.

Activity 2.4

To help you internalise Scott's typology of documents by authorship and access, try to use it to make a rough classification of the documents which are presently in your home. First list the various types of document (personal letters, library books, newspapers, committee papers, study materials etc), then try to classify them.

My comment

Whether you found that the documents you hold at home covered most of the available categories probably depends on the extent to which your professional interests spill over into your home life. I hope you did not have any documents of type 9 in your home (documents protected by the Official Secrets Act). However, regular stories of briefcases stolen from cars suggest that such documents do frequently make the journey from office to home!

Now we turn to the discussion of documents as the sole source of data, and to a reading of a rather different kind.

❏ Documents as the sole source of data

Much useful documentary research is of course done in association with other research approaches. For example, we saw that the research into school governing bodies used to illustrate the case study approach included a study of governing body minutes over a period of years. When documents are the *only* source of data, however, the study probably relates to a period somewhat remote in time, and it is difficult to find examples of purely documentary research which have the ring of immediacy.

An example of some documentary work on the history of the King James's Grammar School in Almondbury is given by Hinchcliffe (1978). His exploration of documentary evidence evokes the charm of the past and, like most documents which give us an inkling of the thoughts and behaviour of people of former times, has a certain fascination. Another writer who has made good academic use of this fascination is Burnett (1982). His *Destiny Obscure* takes the autobiographies of 28 working people, written between 1820 and 1920, and presents extracts from their accounts under a number of social themes. If you have time, the section on Education, with its scholarly introduction, could prove stimulating to your own research ideas (pp.135–211).

However it must be admitted that most documentary research, focusing on contemporary or near-contemporary documents, lacks the charm of the past and can become a laborious and sometimes tedious task. It is important therefore to realise the benefits of documentary research.

❏ Strengths of the documentary approach

Documentary research can:

1. Be a relatively low cost form of research, (depending on the location of relevant material).

2. Bring together previously unrelated material which illuminates a topic.

3. Enable enquiry into past events/issues where there is no access to contemporary participants.

4. Increase knowledge by bringing to light material which has not previously had wide circulation.

5. Be an 'unobtrusive' method of research (see Section 2.5.).

6. Be of value in supplementing data collected by other means (e.g. the study of committee papers supplements observation of meetings).

Equally, of course, documentary research has its pitfalls.

❑ Weaknesses of the documentary approach

1. Documents and records are unlikely to have been prepared for purposes similar to those of the researcher.

2. The acceptability of a document as a source of evidence cannot be taken for granted. It is essential to appraise the authenticity, credibility and representativeness of any document used in research (Scott, 1990). (This point is further developed in Chapter 3, Section 3.4.).

3. It may be difficult to establish the principles underlying classifications in official documents.

4. Administrative documents are not neutral reports of events. They are shaped by political context and by cultural and ideological assumptions.

Finally, as in other sections, we look at the resources which the 'pure' documentary research approach requires.

❑ Resources needed for research based entirely on documents

These are:
(a) access to specialised libraries/archives, as appropriate
(b) time available for what may be lengthy searches

(c) patience and thoroughness in unearthing relevant material
(d) good interpretative and writing skills on the part of the researcher, to bring the material to life for the reader of the research report.

If you would like to explore the subject of documentary research further, and think it may have particular relevance for your own project, I suggest you read the whole of Scott's book, *A Matter of Record* (1990) to which I have been indebted in preparing this section. You will also find further help in Chapter 3, Section 3.4 which deals with records as a research tool.

2.4 Experimental approach

The experimental approach to research is not well adapted to the investigation of educational management practice. Nevertheless experimental research has been and is widely used in other areas of social enquiry. It is important to appreciate the principles on which it is based.

❏ Definitions

The *experimental approach* to research puts forward a hypothesis of causal relationship between variables, that is, it is predicted that a change in one thing will produce a change in another thing. An *experiment* is a means of collecting evidence to show the effect of one variable upon another (Miller, 1984, p.5). It involves making a change in the value of one variable — called the independent variable — and observing the effect of that change on another variable, called the dependent variable.

Experimental observations are the fruit of 'experience planned in advance, and designed to form a secure basis of new knowledge' (Fisher, 1951, quoted in Selltiz et al. 1965).

❏ Requirements of experimental research

An essential feature of experimental research is control over the conditions of the experiment by the researcher. The model is that of the physical sciences as when, for example, the expanding effect of heat on a metal bar is observed under laboratory conditions. In research involving human subjects it is however rarely possible for investigators to undertake true experiments. Uncontrolled variables intervene to cloud the experiment. This is best illustrated by means of an example.

The prediction could be made that sleep deprivation causes an increase in reaction time to visual signals (Miller, 1984, p.5). In Miller's suggested case, an experiment would involve one half of a group of subjects in being deprived of sleep for one night while the other half were allowed to sleep normally. In the morning the reaction time of each subject would be measured.

However, uncontrolled variables may intervene. Members of the control group who are 'allowed to sleep normally' may in fact have their sleep disturbed for a variety of reasons. Traffic noise, for example, might be an 'uncontrolled' variable.

Every effort must be made to minimise or 'hold constant' the effect of other variables in experimental social research, and the major key to this must be the random selection and allocation of subjects to the experimental and control groups. Another way is by 'matching' pairs of individuals who have a number of characteristics in common, and dividing them between the two groups. These are ways of apportioning out or nominally 'controlling' for extraneous variables. However it is not possible to eliminate all uncontrolled causes which may influence the result of an experiment.

❑ Strengths of the experimental approach
1. It enables the establishment of (relatively) secure causal relation-ships.

2. It identifies simple connections between variables, which can readily be understood and may be replicated.

❑ Weaknesses of the experimental approach
1. Simple experimental designs cannot effectively cope with multiple causality.

2. It is narrow in scope.

(If the causal relationship tested proves not to exist, the experiment provides no alternative insights.)

❑ Resources needed for experimental research
Painstaking research design, with the opportunity for extensive pilot work (to get the flaws out of the design).

Complete confidence in the researcher by those enabling access, and a high degree of cooperation in fulfilling the conditions which the researcher's experimental design requires (see the case from Cohen and Manion, 1980, quoted at the end of this section).

❏ Use of the experimental approach in educational research

Although widely used in educational psychology, the experimental approach in its pure form is not usually seen as appropriate for institution-based education research (in school or college). Cohen and Manion (1980, p.188) suggest that in educational settings most empirical studies are quasi-experimental rather than experimental. The groups with which an education researcher works are likely to be 'intact' groups, i.e. groups constituted by means other than random selection, such as members of a class, or the staff of a college department.

In studies of educational management it is unlikely that experience can be 'planned in advance' (in Fisher's terms). Some pilot studies of management innovations might be loosely termed experiments, but they lack certain essential features. For example, the introduction of local financial management for UK schools was piloted in a few authorities in the late 1980s, but no specific 'control' group was studied over an equivalent period. The only basis for comparison were the other LEAs not included in the pilot study.

Activity 2.5

Consider, and list down, some of the ethical and practical problems of establishing a control group for a single-handed experimental study in educational management. Take as your example an experiment in the introduction of teacher appraisal.

My comment

The main ethical problem which applies to any use of 'control' groups is that if an experimental innovation is presumed to be of benefit to the experimental group, how can withholding this benefit from the control group be justified? In the case of teacher appraisal, this has been publicly introduced as a developmental initiative for staff, from which all will benefit. Why should some teachers be left out, for the sake of an 'experiment'?

In a particular institution it might however be the case that resources permit the appraisal of only a proportion of teaching staff in a given year. In this case, the would-be experimental researcher would hope to have some say in who was appraised and who not. The aim would be to establish, as far as possible, 'matched' pairs in experimental and control groups, of teachers with similar seniority, length of service, range of responsibilities and any other variables seen as relevant to the analysis to be made.

In practice, the division of staff into appraised and un-appraised is likely to be a management decision based either on expressions of teacher preference or convenience of time-tabling. If the researcher had to analyse the experiment's outcome by studying two groups of staff, one of which had willingly undergone appraisal and another which had equally willingly foregone it, it would, to say the least, be difficult to evaluate the difference made to staff development by appraisal. As in Miller's 'sleep' experiment referred to at the beginning of this section, uncontrolled variables could cloud the experiment, the main uncontrolled variable in this case being teachers' predisposition or otherwise to value the appraisal experience.

As a cautionary tale illustrating the difficulties of experimental research in educational settings, I conclude this section with a quotation from Cohen and Manion (1980, p.160). They cite a classic case of the difficulties experienced by a graduate student (from the University of Leicester). It indicates how many extraneous variables may be outside the experimenter's control in even a simply designed experiment such as 'before and after' (pretest–post-test) testing. The purpose of the enquiry, in six secondary schools, was to evaluate the use of archive materials in the teaching of history, through the use of a particular set of teaching materials.

> The pretests were taken by 158 children in six schools ... not all the children who had taken the pretests either used the Unit or took the post-tests, which were completed by only 72 children. Without the backing of a national body ... one's status and purpose are suspect and offers of assistance are not readily forthcoming ... The six schools used were the only ones to offer assistance after a request had been sent to most secondary schools in [the county]. This had two main results. In the first place, the need to work with any school classes whose teachers offered to co-operate in order to obtain a sample of adequate size meant that variables such as age, intelligence, previous learning experiences, etc. could not be controlled. ... Secondly, although all classes used the same materials, it was impossible to insist on common teaching patterns, equal provision of additional resources, similar periods of time devoted to each section of the materials or the use of control groups. Drop out during the use of the materials due to natural causes such

as illness or a teacher's practice of allowing unrestricted choice of work patterns also reduced the size of the sample, resulting in different sample sizes for pre- and post-tests.

If you would like to read more about experimental research, Selltiz et al. (1965), Chapter 4, is still one of the best sources. See also Cohen and Manion's (1980) Chapter 8, on Experiments and Quasi-Experiments.

We turn now to a form of research which is the polar opposite of experimental research.

2.5 Non-reactive approach

This approach to research is the exact opposite of the experimental one. Instead of the researcher seeking to 'plan experience in advance', as Fisher (1951) suggests, the intention of non-reactive research is to use as data experiences and behaviour which are totally undisturbed by the research act. The commonly-used expression of 'a fly on the wall' sums up the idea that life flows on normally when people are unaware of being observed.

Experimental research *sets out* to be 'reactive', that is to have an effect and to monitor that effect. Other forms of research already discussed are also, if to a lesser degree, 'reactive'. The presence of a survey or case study enquirer, the task of completing a questionnaire, focus the attention of research subjects in particular ways, so that the information they provide and the behaviour they exhibit is to some extent influenced by the research enquiry. Even documentary research cannot claim to be entirely non-reactive. Certain documents, if originally prepared on the understanding that they would at some time be open to scrutiny, can be said to have been drawn up in anticipation of an unknown reader. (Have you ever re-phrased a written comment on a child's work or behaviour, knowing that a parent would read it?)

Although all social research is to some extent reactive, we can appraise and define a non-reactive approach to research.

❑ Definition

A non-reactive research method is one which gives priority to minimising disturbance to the subject of study.

Two main forms of deliberately non-reactive research are to be found in the literature: unobtrusive measures, and covert research.

❑ Unobtrusive measures

Webb et al. (1966), in a classic text, discuss among other techniques how data may be acquired on a 'physical traces' basis which can be claimed to be entirely non-reactive. They cite the measuring of erosion of flooring around particular museum exhibits, or the accretion of finger-marks on certain pages of library reference books, but such measures have limited applicability. Webb et al.'s text pre-dates the technology which enables unobtrusive 'bugging' of rooms or buildings, but they discuss equally dubious methods of obtaining data, such as concealment under beds or in cupboards. *Unobtrusive Measures* is entertaining to read, but it raises a number of serious ethical issues.

❑ Covert research

This term is generally used for forms of enquiry where the researcher does not conceal his or her presence, but assumes a disguise or covering role which conceals the intention to acquire data. The approach has on several occasions been used by professional researchers in situations where overt access might be difficult to negotiate and maintain, for example in 'closed' environments such as prisons or places of long-term psychiatric care, or in the study of various forms of deviant behaviour. Several examples of this kind of clandestine research are reported in Bulmer (1982).

The researcher who undertakes covert research is of course at risk of (legal or illegal) retribution if the research cover is 'blown'. Even if not discovered, their bringing of covertly acquired knowledge into the public domain through publication of books or articles is perceived by some as unethical.

Activity 2.6

If you could devise a way of obtaining 'unobtrusive' data on, for example, parents' disciplinary methods when assisting with school outings, would you regard yourself as ethically justified in publishing this in anonymised form, without notifying the parents concerned?

If you were able systematically to observe and record your colleagues' pattern of interaction in, for example, senior management team meetings, and you were able to do this under cover of your own membership of the team, would you feel entitled to use these data, in anonymised form, as part of a research report?

My comment

Responding to these questions may have given you some notion of where you draw the line between ethical and unethical research behaviour. Both cases would technically infringe the notion of 'informed consent' by research subjects, which I shall discuss in Chapter 4.

❑ Minimising the disturbance caused by research

Although the forms of non-reactive research so far discussed in this section are ethically problematic, the principle of minimising the disturbance caused by research is both ethically and investigatively sound. Conducting research in a non-reactive *style* means designing research instruments, or setting up research circumstances, which do not of themselves pre-determine or change the data acquired.

I have already referred in this text to the unwanted phenomenon of 'interviewer-pleasing'. This effect, of the interviewer giving the replies which an interviewer seems to expect or prefer, is produced when the investigator seems to embody certain values, or openly expresses them during the enquiry. A notable example was the first phase of the Nottingham-based Child Development Study (Newson and Newson, 1976). The first wave of this longitudinal survey was carried out by a team combining health visitors and university personnel. The health visitors collected data on mothers' care of children in the first year of life which were markedly different — and closer to perceived 'best practice' — than that collected by other members of the survey team. Re-selection of the survey interviewers eliminated this interviewer-pleasing effect in later waves of the study.

Another way in which non-reactiveness is aimed for in research is in the design of questions, for interview schedules or self-completion questionnaires. 'Leading' questions, which assume particular answers, are not conducive to candid responses. All 'closed' questions (which offer a choice between pre-determined answers) should provide a wide and evenly worded range of possible replies.

In observation-based studies, disturbance to the situation observed can be minimised by the repeated presence of the observer, by the observer playing a low-key role in any interaction with the observed, and by the use of non-intrusive means of recording data. From experience I can say that the presence of the average film crew in any classroom or school situation provides the exact opposite of these desirably non-reactive circumstances. The accuracy of any so-called 'fly on the wall' school or college documentaries must be called into serious question!

A note on 'action research'

'Action research' as a distinctive research method is not explored in this text. Action research, which came into vogue in the UK in the 1960s and 70s, is a research method which still has its advocates, but I am not among them. Essentially, it involves researchers and practitioners in team working, to introduce an innovative programme of some kind into an institution and monitor its impact, making adjustments and changes to the programme as it continues to be worked on. Advocates of action research believe that little can be achieved 'if only one person is involved in changing his (*sic*) ideas and practices. For this reason, cooperative research tends to be emphasised and encouraged' (Cohen and Manion 1980, p.1978). Action research has the aim of bringing immediate improvement to an ongoing programme rather than making an assessment of a situation as it stands (as other forms of research tend to do), then providing recommendations for future change. My problem is that interventionist tinkering of this kind does not equate with my view of research.

◎ Reading 5

*Cohen and Manion (1980) give an even-handed assessment of the strengths and weaknesses of action research in their Chapter 9. It is included in **Part II**, p.116, so that you can make your own judgement of its possible applicability for your research project. Another useful source on the subject is Carr and Kemmis (1993).*

Having worked through this chapter, and tackled the *Activities* it includes, you should now be able to summarise the principal features of the research approaches discussed. I hope you can see that they all have their strengths and weaknesses. In planning your own research you may be aiming to use a number of different approaches.

Your research design should try to build on the strengths and minimise the weaknesses of the methods you use. Your final report should make some appraisal of how far you think you have been successful in this.

Be comforted by the assurance that nobody's research is perfect!

3 Research tools

Research tools are the means by which different approaches to research are operationalised. In this chapter I shall examine in more detail the four main tools for social research: questionnaires, interviews, observation, and the use of records or other documents. The chapter will conclude with a consideration of the use of diaries as a research tool.

No *Activities* are included in this section. The purpose of activities is to help you relate what you are reading to your own research plans. But before using any or all of the research tools discussed here, for your own research, you will need to follow up the relevant parts of this text with further reading, which is either referenced in my text or listed at the end of *Part I*. Where possible, I have included extracts from the work of other writers in *Part II*.

3.1 Questionnaires

❑ Distinctive features of questionnaires

The essence of a questionnaire, as a research tool, is that it is in the hands of the respondent, and is completed by him or her.

This is the fundamental difference from an interview schedule, which may be similar in format but remains in the hands of the interviewer, who completes it on the basis of information supplied by the person interviewed.

A questionnaire empowers the respondent, who may read all the questions before completing any, may complete and return the questionnaire at a time convenient to themselves, or fail to complete the questionnaire at all. (Partial exceptions to these general statements are questionnaires distributed to 'captive audiences', such as pupils, students, or participants in a meeting, who are asked to complete and return the questionnaire on the spot). Although a person being interviewed may also decline to answer particular questions posed by the interviewer from the interview schedule, control over the research encounter remains mainly with the interviewer, once the interview has been acceded to.

❏ Effective use of questionnaires

Four things are essential to the effective use of a questionnaire as a research tool.

1. Ensuring that the questionnaire will be clear and comprehensible to desired respondents.

2. Getting the questionnaire into the hands of the appropriate respondent.

3. Motivating the respondent to complete and return the questionnaire.

4. Making effective administrative arrangements for the return of questionnaires.

These four important points are more fully discussed below.

❏ Content and style of questionnaire

An experienced researcher, writing on the subject of questionnaire design, has said 'The only qualifications needed for success are the ability to think clearly and to ask plain questions in simple unambiguous terms' (Evans, 1984, p.49). For many of us, our first attempt at designing a questionnaire shows that we appear to lack these basic qualifications! Here is some good advice from Moser and Kalton (1971, pp. 319–20):

Simple language

In choosing the language for a questionnaire the population being studied should be kept in mind. The aim in question wording is to communicate with respondents as nearly as possible in their own language. A survey of the members of a particular profession, for instance, can usefully employ the profession's common technical terms; not only are such terms part of the informant's common language, but they also normally have a single precise meaning, unlike everyday terms, which particularly to professionals are often vague and ambiguous.

Technical terms and jargon are, however, obviously to be avoided in surveys of the general population ... Question designers ... are not always the best judge of the simplicity and clarity of their own questions. The reactions of typical respondents — not only of their own professional colleagues — should be sought (informally and in pre-tests) to ensure that the questions are comprehensible.

This passage highlights two important issues in questionnaire design; the respondent's need to understand the questionnaire and find it relevant to his or her knowledge, experience, and expertise; and the researcher's need to try out the questions before sending out the questionnaire in its final form.

🔘 Reading 6
Still on the subject of clarity, turn now to **Part II**, *p.132, and read the passage on Problem Questions. (Kane, 1985, pp. 78–79) Then return to this text.*

My comment

The examples given in the passage you have just read are USA derived, but they are equally relevant to UK research. I suspect that Kane has drawn her example questions from student projects! You should come back to this extract if you draft a questionnaire of your own.

Another central issue in questionnaire design is the need of the researcher for relevant information. You may have framed a clear and unambiguous question, but will the answer to it tell you what you need to know? Questions that are 'superfluous to the main task' (Bell, 1987, p.58) should be abandoned, but it is equally important to ensure that questions seeking vital information are not omitted. The best check for this is, again, some form of pre-test or pilot study.

❑ Piloting
Questionnaires are a research tool which perhaps more than any other need a pilot run. It is not until you have some completed questionnaires available for analysis that you can be sure your research needs are going to be met by the information you have asked for.

Ideally a pilot study tries out the research tool on respondents who would be eligible to take part in the main study, that is, they have the same characteristics as the population to be approached. The experience of pilot study respondents is used to improve and amend the questionnaire before sending it out to the main research population.

In large scale studies, extensive piloting may be possible, and changes to the main study questionnaire will be made on the basis of which questions are left unanswered or answered confusingly.

In smaller pilot studies it may also be possible to ask respondents to give comments on perceived strengths and weaknesses of the questionnaire. Bush et al. (1993) piloted their questionnaire to staff at grant-maintained schools with 12 pilot respondents in this fashion, and the researchers were able to fine-tune the eventual main study questionnaire on the basis of respondents' notes and an analysis of their completed questionnaires.

Any piloting, whether of questionnaires or interview schedules, gives a last opportunity to spot whether some vital question has simply not been included.

❏ Modes of distribution

Self-completion questionnaires must find their way into the hands of appropriate respondents. There are several ways of getting them there, the choice of which depends on the kind of coverage required.

The most usual method of distribution is by post, and this presupposes that both the names and the addresses of identified and eligible respondents are known. (It may be useful to note that in the methods literature, postal questionnaires are often indexed as 'mail surveys'. Two definitive and much-quoted papers on the subject are Scott's 'Research on Mail Surveys' (1961) and Deming's 'On Errors in Surveys' (1944).

Questionnaires may also be handed out at appropriate gatherings or meetings, for *in situ* completion. An example of this type of questionnaire, which needs to be short and simple, is the 'evaluation form' which conference or seminar participants are often asked to fill in, as feedback on the material used. Surveys of this kind are essentially local to a particular venue or occasion.

Thirdly, what may be termed 'catch-as-catch-can' surveys physically put questionnaires into the hands of respondents by having them distributed at gateway points in public places (for example, London Transport questionnaires to passengers may be handed out at the entrance or exit to underground stations), or the questionnaire may be printed in a magazine or newspaper.

Of these methods, postal distribution (or personal delivery) to named persons is the only way of ensuring that a particular and selected sample of individuals receives the questionnaire. However, it cannot ensure that these individuals complete and return it!

❑ Motivation of respondent

Taking the case of the questionnaire received by post, the respondent is most likely to complete and return it if it is made clear:

  (a) why they are individually approached for this information
  (b) what use will be made of the information
  (c) that the research enquiry is being effectively administered and that the researcher is a competent and suitable person to conduct the enquiry

These are essential features of 'motivation to complete', and must be addressed in a covering letter or preamble. Further motivation may come from the format and (restricted) length of the questionnaire, from any offered incentives to complete and return the questionnaire, and from clear instructions about means of return of the questionnaire.

❑ Return of the questionnaire

Completed but unreturned questionnaires are useless to the researcher, so the arrangements for return are as important as the questionnaire design.

For postal surveys, addressed and franked envelopes are desirable, with further reiteration of address for return of the questionnaire itself, in case the envelope is mislaid.

Where local or venue-related surveys are concerned, individual pick-up (e.g. by the seminar leader) may be feasible, but in most local or catch-as-catch-can surveys clearly labelled postal bins cater for anonymity and ease of return.

❑ Non-response

We have looked at the question of how respondents generally can be encouraged and helped to complete and return the questionnaire they receive. But whatever arrangements are made, there will always be some non-response. The significance of this is dealt with at length in the research literature. The point to be established, if possible, is: Does the non-returner of the questionnaire differ from the returner in some characteristic which is relevant to the research enquiry? If so, the failure to include data from the non-responding group will bias the survey findings. For example, if an enquiry about head/deputy head working relationships was addressed to both parties at a range of schools, but in the majority of cases only the headteachers completed and returned the questionnaire, this would rob the survey of much of its explanatory power. Findings from a survey will also be biased if non-response is *systematically* linked to some characteristic which has not been pre-defined as relevant to the enquiry. For example, in the above case, it could be that deputy heads who have been in a post for less than five years are the ones who fail to return the questionnaire. This feature of non-response could be difficult to identify.

Any researcher using a postal questionnaire as the main research tool must not only calculate and report on the response rate achieved, but also make some attempt to identify any patterns in non-response, and take these into account when assessing the collected data.

◎ Reading 7

*Turn now to **Part II**, p.135, and read what Hoinville and Jowell (1978) have to say about Coping with non-response. Although these writers are discussing non-response in large scale random samples, you should bear in mind as you read that potential biasing factors are to be found in the responses — or non-responses — to any questionnaire. Then return to this text.*

My comment

The nightmare of getting no questionnaires returned at all is one which besets every small scale researcher. To make sure it does not become reality, the work required for motivating respondents which I have been describing in this section is well worth while. If however there is still substantial non-response, you should do all you can, on the lines that Hoinville and Jowell suggest, to identify the characteristics of non-respondents, and assess what their replies might have contributed to the study.

❑ Research enquiries for which questionnaires are suitable

My discussion of questionnaires as a research tool is far from exhaustive, but it draws attention to features which indicate its suitability or unsuitability for different types of enquiry.

Postal questionnaires are particularly suitable for surveying scattered, specialist populations (for example college principals, careers teachers or any professional of whom there is probably only one per institution). It is far cheaper to cover such a population by questionnaire than by interview, and the specialist role of questionnaire recipients means they will recognise why they as individuals have been contacted. Their educational level also makes a self-completion questionnaire an appropriate form of approach.

Questionnaires can also be used for non-professional populations, but considerable effort is needed to design and test a questionnaire which is comprehensible to all members of a multi-ethnic group, for example a body of parents whose children attend a particular school. As in all forms of survey, the respondent and the researcher need some shared frame of reference or view of the world. (See Chapter 2.1.)

The questionnaire is unlikely to be an effective research tool if a great deal of information is required from each respondent. For most postal enquiries, questionnaires need to be short. Response falls off with lengthy questionnaires. However, Hoinville and Jowell (1977, p.127) dispute this for certain cases, pointing out that special populations whose members know a good deal about the subject of study may react negatively to what seems a trivial treatment, if a complex subject is enquired into by a short questionnaire. They contend that the appearance of a questionnaire is more important than its length.

> The task required of respondents must appear to be easy and attractive. A complicated, compressed layout with little space on a page is almost certain to be less inviting than a longer questionnaire with ample space for questions and answers.

Except in very large-scale studies, questionnaires are not usually the sole research tool. As we have already seen, some interviews may be necessary to compensate for non-response (Hoinville and Jowell, *Part II*, p.135), and interviews are frequently also used to flesh out the relatively slender data acquired by questionnaire.

3.2 Interviewing

❑ Distinctive features of interviews

> *Any interview is a social encounter between two people, but any social encounter is not an interview. Interviews have a particular focus and purpose. They are initiated by the interviewer, with a view to gathering certain information from the person interviewed.*

Interviews may be individually tailored to the circumstances and experience of particular interviewees ('specialised' interviews) or they may be standardised by use of an interview schedule which is administered by the interviewer to a succession of members of an identified population ('structured' interviews). A variant of this kind of interview is the 'semi-structured' interview, which covers equivalent ground with a number of interviewees, but in a less rigourously standardised way than the 'structured' interview. All research interviews are initially devised by the investigator (who is not necessarily the interviewer), to ensure that they will address issues relevant to the research question.

❑ Structured interviews

Structured interviews are still social encounters, and this is where they differ from postal questionnaires, but social interaction is kept to a minimum while the schedule is worked through.

The principle underlying a structured interview is consistency, through the application of a standardised stimulus to the respondent, with the interviewer measuring and recording the responses. It is suited to the conduct of a large number of interviews in which the person interviewed has no foreknowledge of the interviewer, and only limited knowledge of the research in question.

Most large scale surveys use this standardised form of interviewing. The task of the interviewer is to make contact with the respondent, briefly explain the purpose of the research enquiry, persuade the respondent to participate in the enquiry by being interviewed, then to work through an interview schedule using standardised language.

Hired hands

The interviewer needs to have certain important personal qualities which fit them for the structured interview task, but not necessarily to have been closely involved in devising the research enquiry. For this reason, structured interviewing of this kind is often delegated to 'hired hands' (an American term used for interviewers employed by agencies for a variety of survey work). By using hired hands the researcher becomes at least one step removed from the fieldwork, and must make positive efforts to remain in close touch with the work done. If you are interested to read more about the management of surveys using professional interviewers, Hoinville and Jowell (1977) Chapter 6, gives a full discussion of the organisation of such fieldwork. Obviously, the use of professional interviewers is not an option for the single-handed student researcher.

Interview schedules

All structured interviews use an interview schedule with pre-determined questions. As noted during discussion of questionnaires, an interview schedule remains in the hands of the interviewer, who enters the information supplied by the respondent. (Lap computers are used to record replies by some house-to- house interviewers, but the interview schedule principle remains the same).

A greater bulk of material, and sometimes more complex material can be elicited by a structured interview than by postal questionnaire. Personal literacy of the person interviewed is not essential. The interviewer motivates the respondent to continue answering a sequence of questions, one by one. And the interviewer can follow critical paths through a blockbuster schedule, in response to informational cues given by the respondent about age group, marital status, economic activity, educational level etc.

Access still has to be negotiated, but once the interview is agreed, a standard introduction to it will ideally be used.

In a classic standardised interview only the wording on the schedule may be used by the interviewer. Questions may seek factually precise information from the respondent, offering a range of possible answers. These are known as 'closed' questions, and are the kind most commonly used in formal interview schedules. 'Open' questions, to which respondents may reply in their own words, are difficult to record in a structured interview, and survey resources may not permit the analysis of these replies.

Some structured interviews on intimate subjects use deliberately informal wording which is nevertheless standardised and must not be changed.

❏ Semi-structured interviews

The prime aim of a structured interview is to get equivalent information from a number of interviewees, information which is uncontaminated by subtle differences in the way in which it is asked for. The semi-structured interview has a similar aim of collecting equivalent information from a number of people, but places less emphasis on a standardised approach. A more flexible style is used, adapted to the personality and circumstances of the person being interviewed.

◎ Reading 8

In a study which I made with two colleagues of parents' relationships with their children's secondary schools, we carried out a number of semi-structured home interviews (Johnson and Ransom, 1983). Turn now to **Part II**, *p.137, and read the short extract from this work headed* 'The Substance of the Interview'. *As you read, note the ways in which the collection of equivalent information was balanced by the need for flexibility of approach, in order to encourage parents of widely differing personality and circumstances to take part in the research. After reading the extract, return to this text.*

My comment

From reading this brief extract you may have formed the impression that flexibility took precedence over structure in these interviews with parents, and that is certainly my recollection from this sequence of hard-won home interviews. Nevertheless we gleaned a mass of broadly comparable information related to our seven areas of enquiry, and we structured our material in a *'post-hoc'* way by transferring our notes to a fourteen-sheet grid. The sheets were unequally divided between the seven areas of interest, giving most space to the areas of prime importance to the research enquiry as a whole. Each sheet was further sub-divided into particular topics of interest or open comment sections. After each interview we would write up our notes on these grids, slotting our information into the various sections, repeating or cross-referencing it where appropriate. An hour-long interview took approximately three hours to write out in this way. (Johnson and Ransom 1983, p.139).

In other research circumstances when using semi-structured interviews it may be possible to give rather more emphasis to structure and less to flexibility. For example, when Bush et al. followed up their questionnaire survey of grant-maintained schools with a number of semi-structured interviews, their interviews followed the same pattern as the questionnaire, allowing comparison with the data from the survey. Nevertheless each member of the research team was able to probe and develop questioning. In these semi-structured interviews the main flexibility was in the time devoted to each interview. Interviews lasted for between forty-five minutes and several hours (Bush et al. 1993, Chapter 2).

Probing
In fully structured interviews, the help an interviewer may give to a respondent is (in theory at least) fully standardised. It may be limited to the reiteration of questions (using the same words) and the use of standardised probes or prompts. Successful interviewers in structured situations tend to motivate respondents by body language and encouraging noises. In semi-

structured interviews, it is less vital to keep probing standardised, but the underlying aim is still to encourage the respondent to reply without 'leading' them in a particular direction.

◉ Reading 9

*Turn to **Part II**, p.139, and read what Hoinville and Jowell (1978) have to say about **Probing**. Then return to this text.*

My comment

Hoinville and Jowell make passing reference to 'interviewer training', and their book is of course mainly intended for professional researchers. Single handed investigators are unlikely to have any interviewer training, unless they have acquired this in the course of their own professional work. If you have had no training in interviewing you can nevertheless get some experience of techniques of probing by paying attention to the ways in which you encourage pupils or colleagues who are trying to get a point over to you. Do you typically 'put words into their mouth', or do you encourage them through body language, interested noises or questions such as 'What do you mean?', or 'What happened then?'. You may also find it helpful to pay attention to ways in which you try to *stop* somebody from telling you a tale you do not particularly want to hear. A bored expression, dismissive or irritated body language, attempts to change the subject, are the converse of effective probing, and should be avoided in all forms of interviewing. (See 'Rapport', later in this section).

❏ Specialised interviews

We turn now to interviews which are individually tailored for particular role-holders or individuals. Unlike semi-structured interviews, they do not necessarily cover equivalent ground with each interviewee. Rather, they aim to acquire complementary information which rounds out data already available from other sources, for example in case study work (See Chapter 2, Section 2). Specialised interviews are often referred to as 'unstructured' interviews, to contrast them with the standardised 'structured' interviews we have already discussed. But just as all interviews are to some degree social occasions, so they all have some structure, otherwise the interview becomes a free-floating conversation.

Distinctive features of specialised interviews

Non-standardised interviews call on the personal and professional skills of the interviewer, usually either the main investigator or a key member of the research team. In specialised interviewing it is the 'researcher-as-interviewer' who is the research 'tool,', rather than the interview itself. The interviewer must:

possess, and possibly demonstrate, considerable background knowledge of the subject under investigation In cases where it is important to draw out the interviewee's interpretation of a role or situation, the researcher may keep a low profile about his or her own familiarity with the topic enquired into. 'But the interviewer must have some capacity to catch the interviewee's meanings, to perceive the framework within which he (*sic*) is talking' (Dexter, 1970). This capacity is acquired by immersion in the subject through a variety of media. In some interviews, rather than keeping a low profile the researcher will want to demonstrate familiarity with the topic, to assure an interviewee that they are not speaking with a novice who must have everything explained to them from first principles (See 'Rapport', below).

use informed questioning This is a great time-saver in the interview itself, but requires much expenditure of time before the interview. The ability to put key questions to individuals in specialised interviews comes from thorough study of research material already available. The first specialised interview may have something of a 'blank page' approach, but as the enquiry progresses it takes longer and longer to prepare for the next interview, as so many relevant leads are already embedded in the data available. This is one reason why it is undesirable to conduct one specialised interview hard upon another, before there has been time to mull over notes, tape or transcript. (See 'Recording the Data' below).

react with sensitivity to new leads However well prepared the interviewer, specialised interviews can offer unexpected opportunities. Interviewees may make illuminative 'asides' to their main theme, and it is the great strength of the non-standardised interview that these can be followed up. (But see 'Control' below).

Specialised interviews also call on the skills of the interviewee. Being interviewed on a non-standardised basis is not a restful experience. The interviewee may be asked, with or without preparation, to give their own account of a situation, or explain a viewpoint on an issue. Having agreed to be interviewed, the social nature of the specialised interview puts pressure on the interviewee not to take refuge in 'Don't know', or to refuse to respond to particular questions, as they might feel free to do in a structured interview.

Rapport
The onus is on the researcher-as-interviewer to foster this elusive quality. In a

specialised interview it is the interviewer who must establish and maintain a socially acceptable interactive relationship with the interviewee, while still fulfilling the aims of the interview to acquire individualised information relevant to the research. Bearing in mind the effort being asked of the interviewee in contributing to the investigation, the interviewer must ensure that the research encounter proceeds as an interesting and mainly enjoyable experience. A bored, sulky or apparently affronted interviewer will soon reduce an interviewee to silence or impatience. On the other hand, a bored, sulky or apparently affronted interviewee must be coaxed by the interviewer into a more favourable frame of mind if the meeting is to be fruitful for the research.

Rapport is difficult to write about briefly. You may be interested to consult some more extended treatments of the subject in Richardson (1965), Whyte (1960) or Dexter (1970). One essential technique is the use of 'respondent antecedents', as they are technically known. These are the snippets of information which interviewees convey in passing, before the interviewer has reached the stage of enquiring about this particular aspect of the subject. The skilled interviewer notes these without interruption, and is careful to return to the subject by saying 'You've already mentioned... Can you tell me more?', rather than bringing in the topic as if it were a totally new one. This reassures the person interviewed that the researcher is really listening to and interested in what they have to say — a sufficiently rare event in life to supply considerable motivation to continue!

Control

What has been said so far emphasises that the interviewer is the person in control of the interview (whereas, as we saw in Section 3.1. a self-completion questionnaire hands over control to the person who receives it). Although the interviewer aims to foster a spontaneous atmosphere which will encourage the person interviewed in free self-expression, there are certain definite tasks for which the interviewer has responsibility. These include:

- getting the respondent started
- keeping them on track by verbal and non-verbal cues
- getting the interview back on track if it strays too far from the research topic
- maintaining the interest of the respondent (already briefly referred to under 'Rapport')

and, very importantly,

- ending the interview

(I can recall one headteacher who, if I had not shaken her hand, got into my car and driven away, would I think still be talking to me in the car park to which she accompanied me after I had unsuccessfully tried to conclude the interview in her office!)

Space will not permit the enlargement of these fairly obvious points here, but you will find reference to them in the texts I cited about Rapport, notably in Dexter (1970).

Recording the data

The answers to open questions, as noted earlier, are difficult to record in structured interviews. Unstructured or specialised interviews, by contrast, rely almost entirely on open questions, which leave the respondent free to reply in their own words. How are the data they supply to be recorded? A tape-recorder seems the obvious answer, and in many cases both researcher and interviewee expect such a recording to be made. However it must be borne in mind that the resources required for recording and transcribing full verbatim accounts are considerable. Bucher et al. (1956) estimate that one hour of recorded interview requires nine hours for transcription and checking.

Even when a tape-recorder is available and acceptable, some notes will be needed. The researcher may want to check over the list of key points which the interview must cover, to note any 'respondent antecedents' (as described on p. 49) which should be picked up on, jot down a reminder of points which are not fully clear and (possibly) make some condensed notes on matters covered when the tape-recorder is not switched on, either at the beginning or end of the interview or during some 'off-the-record' interlude. Note-taking can also serve as a non-verbal cue to the interviewee, as Dexter (1970, p.57) points out:

> One way for the interviewer to exert some control over the interview and to respond without breaking into a valuable monologue is simply by the way he takes notes. Rapid recording, plus a look of interest, is an encouragement; dropping the pencil altogether shows that the interviewee is off the point.

❏ Research enquiries for which interviews are suitable

There would seem to be few aspects of social research where interviews are an entirely unsuitable research tool. What chiefly regulates the extensive use of interviewing is the cost. Hired hand interviews are financially costly and require supervision and administrative back-up. Specialised interviews make heavy demands on principal researcher's time.

However, structured interviews have proved a most successful method for gathering quantities of the 'equivalent information' which we have defined as the essence of survey. The British Social Attitudes Survey, regularly conducted by Social and Community Research, is an example of skilled standardised interviewing on a large scale. The Survey contributes to the findings of *Social Trends*, published annually by HMSO. In structured interviewing of this kind the social contribution of the interviewer, though limited, serves to elicit more detailed and in some cases more sensitive data than can be obtained by self-completion questionnaires.

Semi-structured interviewing is the style most likely to be followed in small scale research, when it is of greater importance to gain the cooperation of a limited number of interviewees than it is to ensure that the information they give is supplied in a standardised and readily collatable form.

Specialised interviews are of greatest value in exploratory work, such as case studies, where the boundaries and parameters of the topic are not clearly defined, and guidance is needed from insiders about key elements of the topic under study. An example of this kind of enquiry was my own study of the coexistence of public and private education, from the points of view of users and providers of both types of school (Johnson, 1987). Individually tailored specialised interviews were essential to enlist the viewpoints of headteachers of independent schools and the leaders of their various associations, headteachers of maintained schools, local authority administrators and councillors, and a number of families who had, for a variety of reasons, used both independent and maintained schools for their children.

◎ Reading 10

A useful book specifically on interviewing in educational research is the work of that title by Powney and Watts (1987). They discuss in some detail the issues I have briefly covered in this section, but do not give much space to interviews as part of single-handed student projects. Nevertheless their chapter on guidelines is applicable to small-scale as well as more extensive research.

*It includes a checklist for researchers who have to report on a research project with interviews. Powney and Watts' list covers the questions about interviews which readers of a research report may wish to have answered. The list is reproduced in **Part II**, p.141. Read it through now, and remember to return to it when you are planning your own research.*

The next research tool we shall examine is observation.

3.3 Observation

In social research, observation is generally used to record behaviour. It may be employed as a primary method of data collection to provide an accurate description of a situation; to gather supplementary data which may qualify or help interpret other sources of data; or it may be used in an exploratory way, to gain insights which can be tested by other techniques.

In this section I draw heavily on Selltiz et al's (1965) excellent chapter on 'Observational Methods'. I illustrate their analysis of non-participant observation by reference to my own experience of formally observing governing body meetings, and in discussing participant observation I refer you to articles by Nias, Southworth and Yeomans on their observation of staff relations in a primary school. These articles are reproduced in *Part II*, pp. 143–159.

❑ What counts as 'research' observation?
Observation is an everyday activity, but it becomes a research tool to the extent that it:

(a) serves a formulated research purpose
(b) is planned systematically
(c) is recorded systematically and related to more general propositions rather than being presented as an interesting description

and

(d) is subjected to checks and controls on validity and reliability

Although a researcher's observations should be systematically planned and recorded, it is always possible that observations of great significance may be made by chance — the 'serendipity' which may benefit any form of research approach. But if such a fortuitous 'gift' occurs, systematic follow-up observation is needed to make something of it.

Two broad forms of observation have been developed for research: structured and unstructured. In education research, structured observation has most frequently been used for classroom studies, but it could also be employed for the observation of meetings. Williams (1984) offers a useful analysis of types of meeting at which either structured or unstructured observation might be employed.

❑ Structured observation

In structured observation, the researcher sets out to observe only the

$$\left.\begin{array}{l}\text{presence}\\ \text{absence}\\ \text{intensity}\end{array}\right\}\quad\begin{array}{l}\text{of certain clearly specified}\\ \text{types of behaviour}\end{array}$$

For example, in a study of equal opportunities and staff management one might monitor the number of contributions which men and women respectively made to staff meetings, or the number and type of remarks which the headteacher or chairperson addressed to male and female members of staff.

It is obvious that to undertake structured observation, the researcher already needs to know a great deal about the phenomenon under study, so as to be able to determine in advance of the observation session(s) what kinds of behaviour should be monitored to get information relevant to the overall research question.

A research *instrument* must be individually devised for recording the observations, and this must be used by all observers assisting in the study (rather like the interview schedule supplied to 'hired hand' survey interviewers). The observational instrument will ideally be piloted over a number of trial runs. It must specify:

- categories of behaviour to be noted
- what counts as an act of behaviour

(for example, if the chairperson alludes to the presence of a particular participant with a joking comment (as in 'I'm glad to see Mr So-and-So has honoured us with his company today!'), is this the equivalent of addressing a remark to the individual?)

- time units

(structured observations are in some cases recorded at specific time intervals, e.g. every three minutes)

- methods of classifying the behaviour observed

(rating scales or 'all-or-none' categories may be needed).

It should be noted that making a tape-recording or video-recording of the activities observed is only a way of postponing the structured observation activity. It is still necessary to analyse the recording by establishing relevant categories for noting behaviour, deciding what time units, if any, should be applied, and setting up methods for recording, for example, who initiated each 'act of behaviour' and to whom it was addressed.

Like structured interviews, structured observations have the potential systematically to collect comparable information. As a rule, several observers would be employed on the task, either in separate settings or on separate occasions. This presupposes adequate training, to promote reliable standards of observation (See Selltiz et al. 1965, pp.232–3).

Problems of structured observation
These may arise from:

- inadequate definitions of what kinds of behaviour correspond to a given concept
- lack of confidence of observers in their own judgement; overloading of categories to be noted, leading to observer fatigue
- observers' perceptions being distorted by their own needs and values

Although it might be anticipated that the presence of an observer recording formal observations every few minutes would inhibit normal behaviour, it has been found that people rapidly become habituated to the observer's presence and activity, so this is not a major problem.

To follow up in more detail the techniques of structured observation you may like to consult Selltiz et al. 1965, pp.221–234. Single-handed observers should however be wary of heavy reliance on fully structured observation. The data collected may prove slender, and would be open to criticism as lacking checks on reliability. We turn now to a form of observation which is less technical in its style and has more frequently been used in the study of educational policy and management.

❏ Unstructured observation
Unstructured observation is, like all forms of research, still a systematic and planned activity, but it casts its net wider than the 'structured' variety of observation. It is generally used to record the behaviour of a collectivity or group, whether this be in a meeting or a series of less formal activities, even to record a 'way of life'. It is particularly suitable for the study of management meetings which regularly bring together the same group of people. For guidelines on analysis of types of meeting, again I refer you to Williams (1984).

The strengths of unstructured observation as a tool for recording behaviour

Using observation, it is possible to:

(a) record behaviour as it occurs. This is more accurate than the retrospective or anticipatory reports of their own behaviour that respondents might give in interview. If it is necessary to compare what is done with what is said, then both observation and interviewing should be used.

(b) pick up 'taken-for-granted' features of situations that would not be mentioned in interview.

(c) record the behaviour of people who are unable or unwilling to describe it verbally.

In elaboration of point (c), it is important to note that observation is less demanding of the active cooperation of the subject than are other research methods. We have already noted that being interviewed is not a restful procedure. People who might be unwilling to describe at length and in detail their participation in, for example, a governing body meeting, may be quite prepared to allow observation to take place. Even though they know they are being observed, not so much is asked of them as in other research situations. On the other hand, the technique requires a great deal of the observer (see below).

The limitations of unstructured observation as a tool for recording behaviour

- It is least suitable for the recording of irregular and unpredictable situations (for example sudden crises in organisations). The observer, through absence, may miss out on a spontaneous occurrence which would have been of interest to the research. More often, it is likely that the infrequent situation the researcher hopes to observe (for example, a governing body recruiting a new headteacher) may not occur during the available research period.
- It is not economical of the researcher's time. Interviewing may be less costly of research resources than the 'hanging about' which often accompanies the use of unstructured observation.
- The researcher may record and accumulate a great deal of information which subsequently proves to be of little relevance to the research question. Webb et al. (1966) calls this superfluous material 'dross'.
- Some events, and many forms of private behaviour, are not accessible to direct observation.

- Observation is limited by the duration of events. As a technique it can be used only for a few hours at a stretch (and some governing body meetings pushed at the limits of my observational attention!)
- It requires a great deal of the observer. Correctness and accuracy of observation must be aimed for, but checks have shown that selectivity, inaccuracy and omissions frequently occur. This has to be accepted as a possible weakness in all observational studies. In unstructured observation this is in some part offset by the richness of the data acquired but, as noted above, in structured observation by a single-handed researcher the data may be both slender and open to challenge as lacking in verified accuracy.

❑ What is the role of the observer?

There are four choices for the observer of group behaviour:

1. To participate actively in the group observed.

2. To be a member of the group but keep participation to a minimum.

3. To observe without becoming a member of the group.

4. To keep his or her presence unknown to some or all of the people observed.

(For an extended discussion of these four roles, see Gold (1969).

The third role, of the observer who refrains from becoming a member of the group, was the role which I and my colleagues adopted when observing governing body meetings (Kogan et al. 1984). The role is similar to that assumed in 'structured' observation, but our aim was to make as full a record as possible of what went on at each meeting, with a view to relating emerging issues in our accounts to existing bodies of theory (See Chapter 1).

The fourth alternative role for the observer usually entails the use of one-way mirrors or other devices. However it is sometimes combined with the first alternative, when a researcher participates actively in the activities of a group but conceals the research purpose, playing the role of a bona fide member. Some of the most well-known examples of participant observation have been of this kind, notably the much-quoted *Street Corner Society* of W.F.Whyte (1955). We have already considered the unsuitability of covert research of this kind for the study of aspects of educational management. Accordingly, the example of participant observation which I have chosen for you to read took place in a school with the full knowledge and agreement of members of staff whose relationships with one another were the subject of study.

Selltiz et al. suggest four essential questions for an investigator using observation:

1. What should be observed?

2. How should observations be recorded?

3. How can the accuracy of observations be ensured?

4. What is to be the relationship between observer and observed, and how can this be established?

◎ Reading 11

As you read the three articles in PART II, pp. 143, 148 and 154, concerned with staff relations in a primary school, note whether the researchers addressed these four questions, and if so what decisions they made. After reading the articles by Nias (1987), Southworth (1987) and Yeomans (1987), return to this text.

My comment

These three articles are worth reading in sequence because they give a rare account of some of the phases of a research project — the initial idea, its operationalisation in terms of a research design, the arrangement of access, the fieldwork and the negotiation with participants about the form of the final product. You will have noticed that these articles are illustrative of the case study approach as well as of the specific tool of observation.

What of the four questions suggested by Selltiz?

What to observe?
Nias (p.143) explains the focus on 'six schools in which teachers were working well together', and the aim of observing what teachers, headteachers and ancillary staff actually do when they work constructively together; what attitudes they hold to each other and their work, and what kinds of leadership are used in productive teamwork. One advantage of unstructured observation is the possibility of sharpening up on what to observe as the work proceeds. In our governing body study, the relative dominance of headteacher and chairperson at governing body meetings emerged as a focus of attention.

How to record?

Nias refers to fieldnotes taken on the spot, unobtrusively and out of sight where possible, in small note-books. All three researchers followed the practice of recording a full account at the end of each day in the field, and these accounts were transcribed for circulation. Our governing body study (Kogan et al. 1984) followed a similar practice, though our accounts were handwritten rather than recorded in the first instance. After one three-hour governing body meeting I noted that it took me three and three quarter more hours to write my account. In such accounts I found it important to distinguish (as Selltiz et al. recommend, p.213) between statements referring to actual events and statements commenting on or interpreting those events.

How ensure accuracy of observation?

In the case of Nias and colleagues, the members of staff observed were the principal verifiers of the accuracy of observation. Yeomans' article in particular gives a useful account of the processes of 'clearance' which preceded the issue of each case study. Our governing body case study documents were also 'cleared' with the chair of governors, the headteacher, and a liaison figure in each LEA.

What relationship between observer and observed?

Southworth explains how the researchers worked in effect as supernumerary 'supply' teachers in the schools, and what the advantages and disadvantages of this involvement were. This was indeed 'participant' observation, and brought with it the ever-present possibility of 'going native'. As Nias points out, practices which at first seemed novel and noteworthy began to be taken for granted, and it was difficult not to become absorbed in the schools' central concerns, to the neglect of the research question. Researchers found it helpful to discuss 'their' schools with other members of the team, to gain an outsider's perspective.

This concludes my discussion of observation as a research tool.

3.4 The use of records and documents

A document or set of records differs from the other research tools we have discussed, such as questionnaires and interviews. The essence of a document or record is that it already exists in a definitive form. Unlike a questionnaire or interview schedule, it cannot be individually designed to suit a particular research purpose, but must be drawn on as a source of data in the form in which it stands. Existing records, whether public or personal, may of course be examined, collated, or combined to meet a particular research need, but the work is done on data which already exist in written or other form.

❏ First steps in using documents

Essential first steps in the use of records or documents for research purposes are to ascertain:

- what range of relevant documentation exists?
- where it is located and can be accessed?

and, most importantly,

- for what purpose the documentation was originally prepared?

It must always be remembered that what documents record is not a direct transcription of social reality, but a refraction of that reality through the various processes involved in the collection and recording of data (Wiles, 1971, quoted by Scott, 1990). Some sets of documents may appear straight-forward and unproblematic, for example the records of students attending a particular college. However I shall use the example of my own study of a set of such records for a particular research purpose, to illustrate some of the problems which arise in attempting to make use of even this straightforward type of record or archive.

Before considering this specific example, we should revisit Scott's four criteria for assessing the quality of documentary evidence (briefly mentioned in Chapter 2, Section 3), and consider these in more detail. Remember, as you read through these paragraphs on the authenticity, credibility, represen-tativeness and meaning of documents, that what is being questioned is the extent to which documents can be taken for granted as accurate accounts of the events or issues with which they deal. As we work through the four criteria, I will apply them to the example of the minutes of a governing body meeting.

Authenticity and credibility

Is the evidence genuine, and of unquestionable origin? Are we looking at an original document, or a copy? The main problems in using a photocopied document are likely to be illegibility, if the quality of reproduction is poor, or missing ends of sentences or even whole pages if the work has been carelessly reproduced. If however the investigator is trying to use a typewritten copy of (for example) a manuscript diary, this may be more a 'version' than an exact copy. Equally, printed accounts of verbal discussions, such as the Hansard transcriptions of parliamentary debates tend to 'tidy up' the comments made by Members, and may not be a fully accurate record of the verbal exchanges (Scott, 1990, p.206n).

> Scott's point about 'tidying up' verbal exchanges is certainly applicable to governing body minutes, which typically reduce the occurrence of a heated debate to the phrase 'following a thorough exchange of views, the meeting resolved ... etc.' Legibility of minutes can also be a problem. However recently produced, some photocopies are poor in quality, and you must expect to find reading such documents is harder work than scanning printed texts.

If the authorship of a document is crucial to the research, as for example the set of diaries ascribed to Adolf Hitler and discussed at length in the national press in the mid-1980s, then both internal and external evidence must be sought to authenticate the document. Internal evidence might be features of vocabulary and literary style, while for external evidence the investigator might look to tests of writing materials used, characteristics of handwriting, and whether the factual content of the document appears to match already established facts. (The Hitler diaries were eventually found to be faked. See Harris, 1986).

> In our example of governing body minutes, it is unlikely that the authentication processes described here would be appropriate or necessary. Even so, it could be of considerable relevance to your research to know who originally compiled the minutes, and who had the opportunity to amend them before circulation to governing body members. Minutes may appear impersonal but they always bear the stamp of the particular minute-writer, as is very apparent if one meeting in a series of meetings is minuted by a different individual.

Representativeness

Is the evidence typical of its kind, and if not is the extent of its typicality unknown? Assessing this means considering questions of survival and availability. Does a full (and contemporaneously prepared) index of the documents exist? Have some of a set of documents to which the researcher has access been destroyed or removed, either accidentally or deliberately? Have some of them withered away, due to deterioration or decay? We have seen that bias can be introduced to a survey by faulty sampling (*Part II*, p.135, 'Sampling', from Hoinville and Jowell, 1978). In the same way, if it is not known whether the documents consulted are representative of the whole set, then the 'facts' which the documents appear to reveal may be contaminated by the bias inherent in selective survival and availability. 'A single reference to a phenomenon may indicate the start of a trend, or the existence of a pattern, but it may be just historically idiosyncratic'. (Platt, 1981, p.35, quoted by Scott, 1990).

> This criterion of representativeness could be important in a study of governing body work, or that of any other management group. It could be highly misleading to analyse the minutes of a single meeting as representative of the issues tackled by a governing body. When, with my colleagues, (Kogan et al. 1984) I embarked on case studies of particular governing bodies, each of which lasted about 18 months, we not only attended all meetings during that period and examined the terms in which these meetings were subsequently minuted, but we also ploughed our way through minutes of earlier meetings of the governing body, extending back over two years, to put our case study of governing body activity in some sort of developmental context.

Meaning

Is the evidence clear and comprehensible? Problems of literal meaning, that is, the ability to decipher the script and to understand the terminology or dating systems used, relate chiefly to historical documents, so I shall not attempt to apply them to our example of governing body minutes. These problems are well discussed by Scott (1990, pp.28–30), who should be consulted if documents from previous centuries are to be used as research evidence. A more universal problem in the use of records and documents, is the question of interpretative understanding. What do the documents or records convey to the investigator?

One way in which the meaning of documents has been interpreted is by content analysis. In this approach, quantitative techniques are used to assess the significance of particular items within a text. The number of times a particular idea is used, and the number of contexts in which it appears, are taken as measures of the importance of this idea to the author of a document. For example one might make an assessment of the ethos of a school *as conveyed by its brochure*, by exploring the number of references to 'discipline' contained within it. This is a simple example, but content analysis is a skilled and complex process, which Scott (1990) discusses on pp.32–33, and more fully on pp.130–135. Curran (1977) is another useful source on this.

Other analyses of meaning might however leave aside the quantitative approach, and attempt to relate the *intended content* (the meaning which the author of the text intended to produce) to the *received content* (the meaning constructed by its audience). The latter may vary depending on the perspectives and interest of the document's various potential audiences (for example, the differing interests of parents reading a school brochure).

In my discussion of these four quality control criteria, I am greatly indebted to Scott (1990). Scott sets out a systematic approach which should be useful to any researcher coming to documentary research for the first time, or who needs to assess another's use of documents in an unfamiliar area. Such a systematic and questioning approach to the value of available documentary evidence will be particularly important where the study of documents is the only research tool used in an investigation. More usually, documentary study supplements other forms of enquiry, and this was the case in my own study of student records. This formed a small part of a case study of the coexistence of public and private education in a given area (Johnson, 1987).

❏ Using documents to check on interview data

◎ Reading 12
*Turn to **Part II**, p.160, and read my account of studying Further Education student records for this purpose (Johnson, 1993).*

Then come back to this text.

A great deal of work may seem to have a small outcome, but this is the essence of scrupulous research enquiry, and can be a particular feature of documentary research.

❏ Reporting on documentary research
My retrospective account in *Part II* was specially prepared for this text. Although, as we mentioned in Chapter 2, Section 3, on the documentary approach, the study of historical documents can evoke the 'charm of the past', most records which researchers are likely to consult lack this appeal. The task of locating, studying, analysing and commenting on existing records and documents may seem a dull one. Perhaps for this reason, few helpful first person accounts have been published of the use of documents in the study of educational policy and management. In some cases, it is publishers who veto these accounts, as of little interest to the general reader. When Kogan and Packwood compiled their useful book on Advisory Councils and Committees in Education (1974), they furnished a full account of how they had retrospectively explored the origins and workings of the various advisory councils for education (Personal communication from Tim

Packwood). Unfortunately, for our purposes, the publishers reduced this account to a brief paragraph on 'Sources', and a simple list of the official reports studied.

❏ Access to documents

Lists of sources are valuable, but they say nothing about the negotiation of access to these sources. In all documentary research, this is likely to be needed at at least two levels. First, some overall licence to consult the material is necessary, and this may mean acquiring letters of introduction or permission to use specialised library sources. (Documents are sometimes stored in the 'stacks' or 'reserve collections' of large libraries). At a more local level, the researcher must obtain the agreement (and possibly the assistance) of specific guardians of the documents or records, such as librarians, administrative assistants, secretaries, pastoral heads of house in schools, etc. This is an example of the need to negotiate research access at a number of levels within an institution, an issue I shall return to in Chapter 4.

In the case of my study of Further Education student records (outlined in *Part II*, p.160), I first 'cleared' the idea of consulting records with the senior staff I interviewed, got the overall agreement of the college Principals, and arranged a personal introduction to the staff of the administrative offices. My assistant and I were mindful of the considerable intrusion on the personal space of the administrative staff, with whom we then spent several days in close proximity during our examination of the records, making *ad hoc* arrangements about coffee, lunch etc.

It was of interest that no member of staff suggested the students concerned might need to be consulted about the use of their records in the research. Following its completion, I provided summary tables and brief explanatory reports to the staff whose subjective impressions I had been verifying.

Now we turn to Commissioned Diaries, a specialised form of document which can be used as a source of research evidence.

3.5 Commissioned diaries

Commissioned diaries are a tool of research which, like many other tools, can be individually designed to meet a particular research need. These diaries should not be confused with the research diaries which investigators are sometimes urged to complete (Burgess, 1989) providing an *aide-mémoire* for recall of all the research encounters and enquiries they involve themselves in, in the course of a project. Nor are they synonymous with pre-existing, spontaneously generated diaries which, as we saw in Chapter 2, Section 4, can sometimes be drawn on in documentary study.

> *Commissioned diaries are records which an investigator asks an informant to compile and produce to assist in the research enquiry.*

My discussion of commissioned diaries draws chiefly on Zimmerman and Wieder (1977) and also on material which I prepared for a residential workshop for distance learning students (Johnson 1990 — Unpublished).

❑ Essential preliminaries to the use of commissioned diaries as a research tool

First, the investigator must carefully consider whether the information to be sought by commissioned diary is essential to the research, and could not feasibly be obtained in any other way.

Commissioned diaries aim to produce an annotated chronological record of a 'log', rather than an intimate journal. The agreement to keep a diary represents considerably more of a commitment by the diarist in time and effort than completing a questionnaire or responding to a standardised interview. Securing the cooperation of the diarists is a problem to be faced. In well-funded projects a fee may be offered, but this is not usually the case.

The diarists must be clear what they are being asked to do, and why. If not fully in sympathy with the task, they will probably not complete it properly. 'Reluctant subjects ... rarely provide usable data' (Bell, 1987). (Later in this section I have more to say about the creation of a relationship of trust as a feature of the successful commissioning of diaries).

Each investigator must devise a set of instructions for potential diarists which are congruent with his or her own research interests.

The form of the diary request and instruction must be fitted to the requirements of the field setting and the characteristics of informants. Diarists must be of a certain educational level to understand and complete the diary.

❑ Research uses for commissioned diaries

As you can see from the imperatives listed above (drawn mainly from Zimmerman and Wieder 1977), commissioning a diary necessitates a lot of groundwork. The investigator needs to be clear exactly what use will be made of completed diaries.

If the diary is simply to be used as a contemporary document for analysis, it is essential to decide how the information will be analysed *before* the diary format is designed. If not, the investigator will have completed diaries to deal with which are indistinguishable from other pre-existing documentary evidence, in that they have not been compiled to meet the needs of the current research.

Commissioned diaries are sometimes intended for the investigator's subsequent use as a basis for intensive interviewing of the diarist. The diary interview (see Bell 1987, Chapter 9) converts the diary into a question-generating device. (But see 'Weaknesses of Commissioned Diaries', below).

Alternatively, informants are sometimes asked to keep diaries *after* being interviewed or observed at work. Hilsum and Kane (1971) in an investigation of the teacher's day, observed teachers' work in school hours. They also asked the teachers to keep a 'diary' record of work done in out-of-school hours on schooldays, at weekends and during holiday periods. Without this diary data, it was felt that the picture of teachers' work would be wholly incomplete.

❑ Strengths of commissioned diaries

- The researcher is not involved in making the observations recorded as data — the diarist supplies an extra 'pair of hands'.
- Data can be collected during unsocial hours.
- The investigator is invisible in the situations being recorded, so does not disturb them. (However, the diary approach is not entirely non-reactive. See 'Weaknesses', below).
- The diary offers the possibility of researching topics which would otherwise be impractical.
- Diaries can produce descriptive findings tied closely to the fine detail of daily activities.
- The diary in conjunction with the diary interview is an approximation to the method of participant observation.

❑ Weaknesses of commissioned diaries

- When used as the basis for diary-interview, a 5 or 10 page diary has been known to generate over 100 specific questions, needing 5 hours of interview!
- There will be variation in the depth and detail reported in diaries.
- Diarists' descriptive language is not standardised, so there may be problems of meaning and interpretation.

- De-briefing or subsequent interview, even if not originally intended, may be essential to aid understanding or check on consistency of diary material.
- Persons who consent to be diarists may be a-typical of others in the same setting.
- Interest in filling up the diary may cause the diarist to modify the behaviour the diary is intended to record. (Oppenheim 1966, p. 215).
- The diary could be a complete fabrication.

❑ Motivating diarists

Just as investigators need to be sure they really need the diaries they are going to so much trouble to commission, so the diarist needs encouragement to undertake and complete the task.

Zimmerman and Wieder (1977, p.488) relied on three things to 'motivate a reasonable conscientious effort'.

> First, there was the personal relationship to one of the research assistants, i.e. they were helping the assistant to 'do his (*sic*) job'. Secondly, the research assistants checked the diarists' progress within the first few days to encourage the writers to make regular entries and to deal with any questions. Thirdly, there was the factor of the fee ... [10 dollars was paid to each diarist] and the fact that the task would not be complete and the fee paid until there was an interview completed based on the diary materials.

This quotation refers to a fairly large scale study, funded by the United States Department of Justice. It reflects the authors' view that 'the effectiveness of the diary method ... is undercut if all that is collected is the diary'. (p.488). For them, the subsequent diary-based interview is the main object of the exercise.

Other researchers have had different priorities and a different scale of resources. Hilsum and Cane were first and foremost concerned to motivate their teacher-subjects to allow them to carry out effective structured observation of the teacher's day in school. All their effort was put into negotiating satisfactory access for this. The request to supplement observation with diary information was subsidiary, but benefited from the thorough groundwork put into negotiating observation access.

◎ Reading 13

*The reading I have chosen from Hilsum and Kane (1971) for **Part II** deals with this negotiation of observation access rather than with the detail of the diary exercise* *which observed teachers were asked to carry out. However, you will find an example of the out-of-school record or 'diary' at the end of the reading. Turn to **Part II**, p.163, now and study Hilsum and Kane's account of their research preliminaries. Then come back to this text.*

You can see from the out-of-school record form included with the reading that Hilsum and Kane were not asking their diarists for descriptive detail. Teachers had the fairly straightforward but repeated task of calculating the time spent on different aspects of job-related activity, during out-of-school hours (evenings, weekends and holiday periods). The important thing was that teachers should have sufficient confidence in the researchers to do this accurately, without exaggeration or distortion.

Hilsum and Kane report that 185 out of a possible 197 diaries were returned complete. This response, together with the observation data which they collected, was viewed by the researchers as justification for the months of painstaking preliminary work which you have read about. The relationship of trust which Hilsum and Kane fostered during their negotiation of access not only motivated teachers to complete the diaries, but to do so, the researchers believed, without falsification of out-of school time spent on professional work. The establishment of such a relationship of trust is a vital step in the successful commissioning of diary data.

In Chapters 2 and 3 I have tried to acquaint you with, or perhaps remind you of, some of the principal ways in which social research can be conducted, and the tools which are useful for this. Chapter 4 will focus on the situation of the single-handed researcher, undertaking a research project in the field of educational management.

4 Doing your project

So now you are going to carry out a research project of your own. I hope all you have studied so far, about research approaches and research tools, has not served to put you off!

In undertaking a project of your own you are joining the research community, perhaps only for a few months or perhaps for a much longer period, if you acquire a taste for this kind of enquiry and decide that you want to continue to make research part of your professional life. Either way, your examiners will expect high standards of you, in a project which is assessed as part of your accreditation for a qualification in educational management. It is important to plan a project which, although small-scale, can respectably stand alongside published research in the same field, and make its own worthwhile contribution to professional understanding.

Guidance on the requirements for your eventual project report, its length, presentational format, referencing and so on, will be supplied by your tutor for your project. My task is to help you think through some of the implications of doing your own project. I hope that this chapter will help you prepare for your task.

4.1 Factors influencing research design

Before we go any further, a general comment must be made about the extent to which any research project can mirror the 'best practice' models of research approach which were discussed in Chapters 2 and 3.

As an experienced researcher I can affirm that each and every research design represents some kind of compromise. de Vaus (1986, p.9) spells out what is involved:

> The course that a piece of research takes will be peculiar to that piece of research: it is affected by the research topic, the technique of data collection, the experience and personality of the researcher, the 'politics of the research', the types of people or situation being studied, funding and so on.

An earlier writer, (Silvey, 1975), has made the same point rather more succinctly, recognising that *a research plan is at best a compromise between the aims of the research, the resources available and the feasibility of the area of study.*

My discussion will take full account of this need to compromise in order to carry through effective and complete research. But successful students will always lay down aims for their research which are *grounded* in 'best practice models'.

There is one other issue we must deal with before getting on to the stages which are common to all small-scale research.

4.2 Research by students who do not work in a school or college

In Chapter 1 I discussed some of the advantages of carrying out research in your own institution, and also some of the pitfalls to be aware of. (You may like to review my remarks at this stage).

Own-institution research is likely to be the norm for student projects. If you already have a role in a school or college you do not have to introduce yourself as an unknown individual to the gatekeepers of that institution, and it is sensible to plan a project which can 'take off' from within your place of work, even if it extends beyond its boundaries. (I will enlarge on the term 'gatekeepers' in my later discussion of negotiating access).

If you do not, however, work in a particular school or college, you need to think carefully what network contacts you nevertheless have in the field of education. If at all possible, your first approach should be to an institution where you are not an 'unknown individual', even if you do not actually work there.

If you are a school or college governor, the headteacher or principal should certainly be prepared to discuss with you whether you could feasibly base your project in their institution. If necessary, they might arrange an introduction to the gatekeepers of some other school or college, more suited to the focus of your research interest.

If you are a parent of a pupil or student in full-time education you should again approach the institution with which you already have a link through your son or daughter.

It is unlikely that you would be undertaking a course on educational management if you had no links whatsoever with education, but if your interest in educational matters has so far been purely academic, and you have never crossed the threshold of a local school or college, your only recourse is to make your initial approach through some intermediary — a teacher, a leader of a parents' association, or a local politician who serves on the education committee.

Remember always that the sphere of your research interest is educational *management*, which means that one way or another you have to penetrate fairly deeply into the heart of an institution where such management is taking place. It may however be possible to do this by gradual stages, as you gain credibility and acceptability in the institution of your choice. If, for example, you gain a 'foot in the door' by going into a primary school to help with beginners' reading, you may need to structure your project around the management aspects of that involvement, by planning a study of the way lay assistants are selected and inducted for their task, how their work is supervised and evaluated, who undertakes forward planning for the temporary visiting help which lay assistants give, and how the work ties in to whole-school development plans for the teaching of reading.

What Silvey (1975) referred to as 'the feasibility of the area of study' will be a prominent part of the research design compromise for any student who does not currently work in education. Any access opportunity must be taken hold of, and your project designed around it to make the best use of what is accessible to you. *Always consult your tutor about whether the enquiry you plan will meet the requirements of project assessors.*

If you are not doing your project in your own institution remember that you have the newcomer's advantage of taking a fresh look at practices which are probably so well known to those carrying them out that they have ceased to reason why and how certain procedures are followed. The issues you raise and the questions you ask may well bring refreshment to a hackneyed routine.

Although from now on I shall be making the assumption that readers *are* already working in schools or colleges, my advice is generally applicable to all student projects.

4.3 Planning and timetabling

For the single-handed student researcher, this timetabling stage must come very early on in the research design. I have put it even before choosing your research topic, because that choice must necessarily be guided by an assessment of the research resources available, especially the resource of time.

Make sure you are clear about the date when your completed project must be submitted in its final written form. Hopefully this deadline is some months away, but the time will pass more quickly than you think.

I suggest that you then make a simple time-chart of the available period, blocking in the school or college term(s) when people you may need to involve in your research are likely to be available, and also noting how your own availability to work in the project is likely to vary over the period. Quite apart from the usual work-load of your job, you may have certain special previous commitments such as attendance at conferences or time necessarily dedicated to particular family events. These will make gaps in your research programme, and should be marked on the chart.

Looking at the period overall, you need a slice of time to set up your research, a period for the fieldwork (of whatever kind), and finally a substantial chunk of time when you can dwell on your data (however acquired) and draft and redraft your project report.

Many factors will influence how long each period can be (not least, the overall time available), but making a rough plan will help you ensure that your fieldwork phase comes at a period in the academic year when any fellow professionals you hope to involve are likely to be accessible (i.e. in term-time). Some forms of fieldwork (for example, home interviews with parents) are of course feasible outside the school or college term, but as a general rule it is best to phase your work so that your reflective period, when you are analysing and writing up, coincides with a school/college vacation.

If this rough timetabling exercise has given you a realistic idea of how many weeks you can allocate for each of the three phases of your research (setting up, fieldwork, analysis/reporting), you are now better placed to choose your research topic. You will realise it must have feasible boundaries and not be over-ambitious.

4.4 Choosing a topic and establishing the focus of the study

Your project has to address some aspect of educational management in school or college. Four broad areas of management can be readily identified:

1. Leadership and strategic management.

2. Managing the curriculum.

3. Managing professional and support staff.

4. Managing finance and external relations.

Your first step could be to decide which of these broad areas seems most likely to be accessible of enquiry, and also to arouse and maintain your interest during the hard slog of research. Make the most of this opportunity for research involvement by choosing a subject which you genuinely want to know more about and which will be directly relevant to your school or college.

If, for example, you are a fairly recently qualified member of school or college staff, not involved with any senior management team or tasks, then the broad area of leadership and strategic management would not seem an obvious choice. Nevertheless, if this is where your long-term ambitions and interest lie, it is worth considering whether an investigation of some senior management role or task would be permitted. Bear in mind, though, that your findings will have to be communicated tactfully to those who have allowed your investigation, as your own junior status may affect the credibility of your findings in the eyes of more senior staff.

Once your broad area of interest and feasible access have been identified, you need to sharpen the focus of your study to a particular manageable topic. You will know you have achieved this when you can, if required to, express the subject of your study in a single sentence, rather than embarking on a diffuse explanation of the management area which interests you. The eventual readers of your report will need that one sentence summary to tell them what to expect. If you are not clear as to the intention and scope of your study, neither will they be!

Figure 4.1 gives an example of the focusing process you will need to go through:

Broad area of research	Specific focus for research	Title and sub-title
Management of teaching staff	Appraisal training	*Learning to appraise: a study of appraisal training provided for senior staff and teachers of one primary school, during the introductory year of an appraisal programme*

Figure 4.1

4.5 Stages of an investigation

I have written elsewhere (Johnson, 1984) on this and many other stages of carrying out a small-scale investigation.

The stages I identify are as follows:

1. Establishing the focus of the study.

2. Identifying the specific objectives of the study.

3. Selecting the research method.

4. Arranging research access.

5. Developing the research instrument.

6. Collecting the data.

7. Pulling out of the investigative phase.

8. Ordering of the data.

9. Analysing the data.

10. Writing up.

11. Enabling dissemination.

(Johnson, 1984, pp. 6–7)

◎ Reading 14

*A larger extract from my paper (1984), including a short section on 'Establishing the focus of the study' is reproduced in **Part II**, p.168, and you can use it to supplement the advice I have space for here. Turn to it now, and take time to read carefully through the 11 stages of investigation which I discuss. Then return to this text.*

My comment

The extract you have just read takes you rapidly through the whole process of carrying out a project. Each section contains a lot of concentrated advice, and you may find it helpful to go back and re-read the relevant section as you work through the stages of your project. However, as I point out in my article, a neat list of stages may give the false impression that they are entirely consecutive and discrete. This is not so. A mental picture is needed of the whole anticipated process before embarking on the first stage, and the stages themselves may well overlap or be tackled out of my listed sequence. Eventual analysis, for example, must be planned for very early on in the study.

You may have noted an apparent omission in my list of stages. It does not include 'Literature Review', which is often a prominent feature of instructions to post-graduate students proceeding to a dissertation or thesis, and is also required of you. My 1984 article did not have space for a separate discussion of this necessary phase of reviewing existing literature, but I briefly mention it under the heading 'Identifying the specific objectives of the study'. As I point out in that section, ideally the student researcher would consult and review all published sources on the chosen topic, early in the project programme. In practice, some highly relevant texts may not come to your notice until you are well into your enquiry. Reference to any such material will need to be integrated into the review you have already prepared.

◎ Readings 15 and 16

*For advice on how to set about your literature search, turn now to **Part II**, p.181, for the reading by Haywood and Wragg (1978) in 'Evaluating the Literature', and to **Part II**, p.185 to consider 'The Literature Review' by Lofthouse and Whiteside. Then return to this text.*

How wide-ranging your literature review is able to be will depend on the libraries and databases to which you have access for your studies. In any case, as Haywood and Wragg point out, you must place some limits on the range of literature you consult. Howard and Sharp (1983) offer useful advice on how to keep the search for relevant literature within feasible bounds.

Experience in carrying out my own research, as well as in supervising many student projects, has taught me that gaining and maintaining research access is a particularly important element of any investigation. So I do not apologise for coming back to a subject which you have already briefly read about in my off-printed article.

4.6 The question of access

In Chapter 1, I pointed out that no-one has an automatic right to embark on formal research, whether in their own place of work or elsewhere. It is a central rule of academic research that gate-keepers of data must give their permission for those data to be collected and analysed for specific research.

The role of a gate-keeper, in the research context, is not just that of a security-checker, who needs to make sure that you intend no deliberate harm to people or property in the area you are entering. A gate-keeper has also to find out if you have a legitimate and acceptable purpose for seeking entry. Why do you want to do your research? Whom will it involve? What resources of time and practical assistance will it draw on? What are you going to do with the data you acquire, and what effect will your work have on the area you are enquiring into? Will your work bring into the public domain matters which are at present private to individuals or the institution where they work?

These large questions may seem somewhat of an over-kill for a small student project, but they are real concerns to which you should have a considered answer ready, even if the questions are never formally put.

❏ Purpose and impact of your research

One valid purpose for your research is to *fulfil the requirements for a higher degree*, and the headteacher or principal of your institution presumably already knows that you are engaged in this distance-learning study. If not, now is the time to impart this information.

It is likely that your advanced study (an investment in self-improvement with which your institution may or may not be giving you financial or other support) has general approval. Even so, you will be well advised to present the educational management enquiry, which is an essential part of that study, in a way that flows with the life of the school or college. Can you show that your topic is one that has already had to be addressed, or will shortly need to be addressed, by professional staff? In other words, *that your research will give insights to a problem with which the school or college is already involved?* In times of rapid educational change, such problems are not far to seek. If your research relates to one of them, even if it makes no great contribution to institutional policy or practice, those taking part in your enquiry will at least have been turning their minds to a live and relevant issue, to which they would in any case have had to give some consideration.

As I indicated in Chapter 2, you are not likely to be undertaking 'action research' in the technical sense, which would mean involving all the people who help you with your research in a defined programme of change, and building in to your study a means of evaluating the changes introduced. (See Cohen and Manion, 1980, Chapter 9, reproduced in *Part II*, p.116). Nevertheless *your project may well draw attention to the need for change in a management process* you have investigated, and make proposals for what that change might be. Depending on your role in the school or college, it may be possible for you yourself to introduce and carry through the changes you propose, or you may have to leave it to others to decide whether change is timely and appropriate.

Being clear about the kind of contribution your research will make to the school or college where it is carried out will help assure any gatekeepers you encounter that participation in the project will not be a negative experience for those who give their time to assist you.

❑ Who are the gatekeepers for your project?

The headteacher or principal has overall responsibility for what goes on in a school or college. They or their appointed deputies must be made aware of the investigation you propose to make, but if yours is a large institution you may want first to 'sell' your project to someone closer to you in the management structure, who can then pass on your access request with the endorsement of their approval.

Research is a necessary management activity which most heads and principals will consider essential to the ongoing improvement of school or college, so any well-prepared and tactfully presented proposal for research is likely to meet with broad approval. However, as I explained in my article, (Johnson, 1984) negotiating access is not a one-step affair. Although the principal gatekeeper may have agreed to let you make a start on your project, there may be others whose approval and support is also needed. Always check with the headteacher or principal whether the Chair of Governors whould be made aware of your research. If the project will involve parents or any other group or individuals external to the school, the Chair of Governors needs to know what you propose. If pupils are to be interviewed as part of the research, parents must certainly be told of this, and you should check with senior staff how this can best be done.

Where college students are concerned, the issue of who gives consent for their involvement is not so clear-cut. It may be the students themselves, but it could be, in the case of mainly 16–18 year-olds, that notification of the project should be sent to their homes. Be sure to discuss this question with someone senior in your institution.

If your research involves a direct approach to parents, the school or college must certainly know of this and be supportive. Your covering letter for any questionnaire to parents should make clear that you have this support, but you should not try to pressurize parents into taking part in your project by stressing that the school 'wants' them to do this. This could produce the equivalent of 'interviewer-pleasing', an effect which I discussed in Chapter 2 p.34. Parents who feel obliged to respond may also try to give the 'right' answers to your questionnaire, rather that the individualised response that you are seeking.

If your research plan includes interviews with colleagues, remember that you should not sidestep other stages of access negotiation by going directly to your colleagues and asking them to take part in your research. Powney and Watts (1987, p.121) outline the possible levels of access negotiation as follows:

> It is not just a question of strolling into a staffroom and asking the various teachers a few questions. For example, to interview a woodwork teacher, approval would probably have to be obtained from:
>
> - the LEA — to conduct research in the authority
> - the head teacher — to make inquiries which might affect the school
> - the head of the woodworking department — to conduct research which might raise issues about the department
> - the woodwork teacher — the interviewer would have to ascertain whether (s)he is willing and has the time to answer questions on the defined topic.

When the interview finally takes place, further reassurance may still be needed, as Powney and Watts (p.129) point out:

> Basically, the courtesies of interviewing are concerned with maintaining the dignity and privacy of the informant. Therefore plenty of time would be allowed to explain the purposes of the inquiry, how the informants can contribute and the length and kind of interview and outcome proposed. Informants should be reassured that the interviewer will preserve their anonymity throughout the inquiry and in any subsequent publication. Reassurances about confidentiality and anonymity may have to be given on several occasions, if the informant seems uncertain, or nervous about talking freely. The interviewer should only make such promises as can be kept.

❑ How can you maintain access?

If you will be carrying out your investigation entirely within your own school or college, and your fieldwork will be lasting for several weeks, remember that you may have to re-negotiate agreement to participate. People who originally agreed to help you may now claim they are too busy, or don't have the information you need. The way in which your enquiries have been received by earlier participants will almost certainly influence the attitude of those who come later in your interviewing or observation programme.

The main inducement you have to offer is your *interest* in what colleagues are prepared to tell you or let you observe, and this attention and interest is what is most likely to reinforce and maintain the initial broad agreement to research access. But remember too the practical points I make in my article (Johnson 1984, reproduced in *Part II*, p.168), about not leaving a trail of disordered files or exhausted interviewees behind you.

Access and ethics are intertwined subjects, so we should now look again at the ethical issues which are inseparable from research, however small-scale.

4.7 Ethics revisited

Ethical decisions are properly made by the individual, but should be informed by the values and experiences of others. (Sammons, 1989, p.56).

Ethical implications of their research are of great concern to most professional researchers. Just as it is important to know the principles of research methods, and adapt them to your own needs, so you should also be aware of the professional approach to research ethics, and consider what the ethical implications of your own research might be.

Sammons (1989) gives a useful list of ethical issues, taken from the guideline code of the International Statistical Institute, and I shall use these issues as sub-headings for my discussion here.

❑ Avoiding undue intrusion

Remember that you are embarking on research enquiry, not investigative journalism. Research into a management issue may not of itself be intrusive, but individuals' self-image and self-esteem are often closely bound up with their work role. Your research is not intended to provoke respondents into discussion of personal relationships or personal characteristics of colleagues which influence the way a particular management task is tackled. If this kind of information nevertheless comes your way, it is up to you to handle it responsibly. (See 'Protecting the interests of subjects', below).

❑ Obtaining informed consent

This is a huge and highly technical issue, but one which is relevant even for small-scale research. In its pure form, informed consent means the person invited to contribute to research:

- is legally capable of giving consent
- is able to exercise the free power of choice (no force, fraud, deceit or duress being applied)
- has sufficient comprehension of the subject matter to make an understanding and enlightened decision

This definition comes from the Nuremberg Code of 1949, drawn up at the time of the War Criminal Trials. You may feel this code is scarcely applicable to small scale research into educational management, but it sets out principles which you need to think about. Like other ethical principles, they are open to a wide range of interpretation.

Legally capable of giving consent We have already discussed the point that minors (pupils) involved in research should strictly speaking have the consent of their parents to take part. Most of your research is however likely to be with adults, who are *legally* capable of giving their consent. The question for you and they to consider is, are they *entitled* to do so? Should their consent, for example, be conditional on the agreement of colleagues, for any reason?

Able to exercise free power of choice Just as parents should not be pressurised into research participation by an over-emphasis on its approval by school or college, so you should not use your (possibly) senior status to 'lean' on more junior colleagues whose help you need. This would in any case be counter-productive, as a coercive approach inhibits rapport and free communication.

Sufficient comprehension of the subject matter On this issue, the small-scale researcher is going to have to make a contextualised decision — or perhaps a series of decisions — about what 'sufficient comprehension' means in a particular case. Genuinely informed consent depends on in-depth knowledge of the possible ramifications and outcomes of a piece of research. Novice researchers may not be fully aware of these themselves, so cannot be fully informative. There is also the question of whether participants really *want* to know the detail of your research. They may find this tedious or unnecessary to their participation. You should adjust the level of your research information to the perceived interest of your intended participant, but make sure that you are telling a consistent and honest story to all the people you approach, even if the amount of detail you give varies. Colleagues may well compare notes, and in your efforts to inform and negotiate access with sensitivity, you may give the impression that the aims of your research are covert rather than declared.

Returning now to Sammons' (1989) list of ethical issues, we must consider the question of:

Protecting the interests of subjects

Unlike the respondents referred to earlier, who may be inhibited by interrogation from a more senior colleague, there are some people who will say anything to anyone! Far from requiring assurances of confidentiality, they regard the research encounter as an opportunity to unburden themselves of all their problems with colleagues, or difficulties in carrying out their own work. Early in my research career I became aware of the need to protect these naive respondents (Johnson, 1976). When people make comments in research interview which if made in the presence of colleagues would get them into trouble, you need to protect them from their own indiscretion by using the material in a tactful or sanitised way, or not using it at all.

Maintaining confidentiality

Confidentiality is a relative concept. Personal counsellors are familiar with the assurance that 'nobody knows — except my friend'. If you are offering confidentiality for research information, you need to be more scrupulous even than those imparting the information are likely to be. In particular, be aware of the danger of cross-fertilising information, that is, making comments to one respondent, based on apparently generally-known information supplied by a previous interviewee, which may in fact be new to the hearer. Unlike some ethical problems which seem most relevant to large-scale research, the cross-fertilisation of information is chiefly a hazard in small-scale, one-institution studies. Make sure it is not you, the student researcher, who puts the 'cat among the pigeons' in a confined space!

Preventing disclosure of identities

In the case of one-institution small-scale enquiries, it may be impossible to conceal the identity of staff members taking part. Even if names are not used, the identity of role-holders is likely to be apparent to in-house readers of your report. Even so, job titles rather than names should be referred to, as this stresses the professional rather than the personalised input which individuals have made to your research.

Pupils and students too are entitled to a veil of anonymity, however thin that veil may be. In an enquiry into school discipline and pastoral care (Bird et al.

1981), under the title 'Disaffected Pupils', my colleagues and I were careful to use pseudonyms for the pupils whose turbulent school careers we described. Although teaching staff might conjecture which of their pupils featured in our report, anonymity meant that the young people whose experience enriched our enquiry could not be called to account for the actions and attitudes they expressed.

In your own research, if you enlist the views of parents, their contributions *must* be anonymised. If you identify the parent you identify the child, who has probably not been a party to your research agreement with the mother, father or guardian. Many parents are apprehensive that criticism of school or college may somehow 'kick back' on their child, and the responsible promise of anonymity means you can reassure them about this, however unlikely you think such a reaction to be.

Utilising identified data

This issue is most likely to arise in the case of documentary research. What you have to avoid is breaching confidentiality at one remove, by making too free use of data to which you have been given access by their custodian but not their subjects. A senior teacher once offered me free access to a store room filled with the records of former pupils at the school. While they were on the roll of the school, those pupils' records would have been carefully protected, but their 'old student' status had, in the teacher's eyes, cancelled any requirement for confidentiality. I had no wish or opportunity to make use of the data which were gathering dust in that store room, but the offer of access brought home to me Sammons' comment that where access is given to identified data, researchers should take into account the likely sensitivity and interests of subjects. It is the researcher's responsibility, 'not only the custodian's, to consider the subjects entitlement to anonymity and informed consent' (Sammons, 1989, p.46).

The ethical provisos I have discussed in this section are important considerations as you embark on your project. But what will be the outcomes of all this research effort?

4.8 Outcomes of research

Before you undertake your own project, the most obvious intended outcome of it from your point of view is probably the report you have to write, in fulfilment of course requirements. This is certainly an important outcome, but

I shall also ask you to think about the impact of your research on colleagues who receive its findings, and the ways in which carrying out the project may develop your own professional understanding.

❏ Your project report

Required parameters for your report are laid down by course organisers. What we need to think about here are ways in which your report can do justice to the work you put in on your project. Remember, you are not just writing an essay or assignment on your chosen research topic — you are trying to make plain to the reader of your report what research-based conclusion you have come to about your topic, and *how you reached that conclusion*. The reader needs to be made aware of:

- the aims of your research
- how you operationalised your research (including the research decisions you took to achieve a workable compromise between the aims of your research, the resources available for its completion, and the feasibility of the area of study)
- the finding of your research and the conclusions you draw from these findings

To take an example which I referred to earlier, let us suppose that the aim of your research is 'To investigate how the process of preparing National Records of Achievement has been integrated into school life'.

The *feasibility* of studying this subject should not be in doubt, because NRAs are required documents for secondary school leavers. However, different local authorities, and different institutions, have responded with varying degrees of enthusiasm to this requirement. Any insider knowledge you have of local attitudes to records of achievement in general, and NRAs in particular, will inform your assessment of whether the investigation will be a straightforward one. Don't abandon your aim (or any similar aim related to any other educational management topic) because you suspect it is not a topic colleagues have hitherto considered very deeply. But bear in mind that your research enquiry may have a developmental role, focusing the mind of colleagues on something that needs doing but has not yet been tackled systematically.

Your *resources* for handling the project also need to be considered. We have already considered the general question of timetabling, so you should know how long you realistically have to set up, carry out and write up your enquiry. The scope of the project's aim could be interpreted on a nation-wide basis, but fortunately it is equally well adapted to a one-institution enquiry, suitable for a singlehanded researcher. Other resources which I hope you will be able to draw on are the goodwill and interest of colleagues generally towards your study-related project, and perhaps in particular towards its subject, if NRAs are perceived as valuable developments in teacher/pupil cooperation.

How you put into practice this particular research aim, of investigating the process of NRA preparation in a particular school or college, will depend on whether it seems appropriate to look at the process in relation to a single cohort of school leavers, or whether the process is known to you to have evolved over a period of several years. If the process has been on-going for some time you might want to undertake some documentary research, and also retrospective interviewing of people involved in earlier stages of the process. You might also arrange to observe aspects of the current process, for example INSET sessions devoted to NRA work, or teacher/student negotiations of the school statement included in the NRA. In any case, make sure that you make clear reference in your report to all that you have done by way of research enquiry — the documents consulted, role-holders and others interviewed, sessions observed, and any other research tools used such as questionnaires and diaries.

The findings of your research, and your conclusions from those findings, may be inseparable if you have used the case study approach for your project. But you should try to use all your findings, including any which conflict with your overall conclusion. In our NRA example you might, for instance, find that senior teachers and form tutors are united in agreeing that NRA preparation has become a valued aspect of pastoral care, alerting school staff to hitherto unknown aspects of students' experience outside of school. Students of a particular school-leaving cohort might however inform you that NRA preparation is a waste of time, because their completed documents were not available in time for college or employment interviews, or if available were not consulted by those who interviewed them. Your conclusions could compare and contrast the two views, and make recommendations as to how the differing perceptions which staff and students appeared to hold about the purpose of NRAs might be reconciled.

Although the example I have worked through may be wide of the mark of your own project aims, my discussion illustrates the elements of aim, operation, findings and conclusions which will make up your report. This will be the principal outcome of your research, but there will be others.

❏ Impact of the project and its findings on colleagues

Will you be sending copies of your report to colleagues? I anticipate not, for reasons of expense and because your fairly lengthy report might not all be of interest to them. As a courtesy you might however want to supply a copy to your headteacher or principal — your tutor will advise you on this. But you certainly owe it to your colleagues to give them some feedback in writing from the enquiry in which they have participated. If you have also interviewed senior pupils and parents, (as might well be the case in my NRA example) then they too may like to know the outcome of your research. A one-page summary of your findings and conclusions would seem most suitable for colleagues, and you will need to consider whether students and parents would value similar written information or whether a verbal summary in a tutorial session with students and/or a school meeting for parents would be more appropriate.

The essence of good communication is to think first of the needs of the recipient, and this should be your guide in all forms of research feedback. Research participants are not a captive audience who must be forced to attend to your research findings and conclusions in their entirety. However there may be aspects of your work which it would be helpful and interesting for them to know of, so this is what you should pass on.

Your enquiry will have been focused on an aspect of educational management, and hopefully it has been concerned with a topic which 'flows with the life of the school', as I indicated earlier in this chapter. If this is so, I hope you will do more than circulate a summary, as feedback to your selected participants. Consult with colleagues about the possibility of making some presentation of the recommendations arising from your work, either by way of INSET for staff generally or in some relevant working sub-group, depending on the nature of your enquiry. In the NRA example there might be a termly meeting of tutors at which your recommendations could be discussed with the Records of Achievement coordinator.

Finally, we look at the possible outcome of your research so far as you are concerned.

❏ Outcome of the project for your own professional development

I hope that studying research methods with the help of this text will already have given you a better appreciation of what is involved in research you read about in professional papers and journals, or in the national press.

Actually carrying through your own project will however inevitably take you many steps further in your understanding of the opportunities and pitfalls of research, and how it can be used to inform management practice. Almost certainly you will know a great deal more about your chosen topic when you complete your research than you did when you began it, and this is why I urged you earlier in this chapter (Section 4) to choose a topic which genuinely interests you. You may well be able to build on the knowledge you have acquired by embarking on a further level of academic study, or use it when seeking promotion, or simply feed it in to your current range of duties.

In doing the research you will have gained many insights into the management of your institution, and these insights will have come to you not only through your work 'in the field' but in the process of negotiating access and arranging dissemination of your research findings. You will also have learned a great deal about any colleagues you have interviewed — and may I remind you once again that you must protect those colleagues from any indiscretions they have voiced in the interview situation. I hope that your research contacts may have taken you beyond your usual range of colleagues, and that you will perhaps have been helped in your research by support staff, students or parents. My own professional life has been greatly enriched by research contacts of this kind, and I am sure your experience would be similar.

I wish you well in your research and any subsequent professional work in the field of educational management.

List of recommended reading

(Full details of all the books mentioned here
are to be found in the references to this text)

Throughout my text I have given you suggestions for books and articles in which you can follow up particular aspects of research. Here I would prefer to recommend books which span the whole field of research methods, and relate those methods specifically to the study of educational management. Unfortunately, no such books exist! This list therefore refers you to books which individually are likely to meet many but not all of your further study needs.

Selltiz et al's *Research Methods in Social Relations* is an excellent and full general text on social research which has stood the test of time. It was written by experienced researchers in palmier days when publishers did not insist on brevity. It coverage is extensive and expert, but it does not focus specifically on education. Copies are probably still to be found in most academic libraries, but it is no longer in print.

If you can't get hold of Selltiz but want a fairly wide-ranging general text on methods, Moser and Kalton's *Survey Methods in Social Investigation* will certainly be available. It deals mainly with survey type research, but has many useful pointers about other research approaches.

Cohen and Manion's *Research Methods in Education* is a clear and well presented methods text which does focus on education (but not specifically on educational management). Some of its advice is a trifle idiosyncratic.

Bell et al's *Conducting Small-scale Investigations in Educational Management* is an Open University course book for students of educational management. This book contains some useful papers but they are nearly all specialised 'further reading' papers which do not combine to present a generalised picture.

Two books which sound, and indeed are, specialised to particular aspects of research are Hammersley and Atkinson's *Ethnography: Principles in Practice* and Hoinville and Jowell's *Survey Research Practice*. Nevertheless, both contain much general guidance which inexperienced researchers can benefit from.

Because of my own interest in research ethics, and my belief that the ethical dimension is an important aspect of all forms of research, I recommend strongly *The Ethics of Educational Research*, edited by Burgess. Unlike the more frequently referenced *Social Research Ethics* by Bulmer et al., which focuses on covert research, Burgess' more recent text ranges widely and expertly over ethical considerations raised by many different forms of research.

Finally, if you want to have a text by you which supplements my discussion of single-handed research (in Johnson, 1984 and in Chapter 4 of this text), you may find Bell's *Doing your Research Project* a useful small book to consult.

References

Anderson, T.R. and Zelditch, M. (1975) *A Basic Course in Statistics with Sociological Applications*, 3rd edn. New York: Holt, Rinehart and Winston.

Bassey, M. (1981) 'Pedagogic research: on the relative merits of search for generalization and study of single events'. *Oxford Review of Education*, **7**, 1, 73–94.

Bell, J. (1987) *Doing your Research Project*, Milton Keynes: Open University Press.

Bell, J., Bush, T.,Fox, A., Goodey, J. and Goulding, S. (1984) *Conducting Small-scale Investigations in Educational Management*, London: Harper and Row.

Berger, P. and Luckmann, T. (1967) *The Social Construction of Reality*, London: Penguin.

Bird, C., Chessum, R., Furlong, J. and Johnson, D. (Ed) (1981) *Disaffected Pupils*, Brunel University.

Blalock, H. (1970) *An Introduction to Social Research*. New Jersey: Prentice-Hall, Inc.

Blalock, H.M. (1972) *Social Statistics*, 2nd edn. New York: McGraw-Hill.

Bryman, A. (1988) *Quantity and Quality in Social Research*. London: Routledge and Kegan Paul.

Bucher, R., Fritz C.E. and Quarantelli, E.L. (1956) 'Tape recorded interviews in social research'. *American Sociological Review*, **21**, 359–364.

Bulmer, M. (Ed). (1982) *Social Research Ethics: an Examination of the Merits of Covert Participant Observation*, London: Macmillan.

Burgess, R. (1989) *The Ethics of Educational Research*. London: Falmer Press.

Burnett, J. (1982) *Destiny Obscure*. London: Allen Lane.

Bush, T., Coleman M. and Glover, D. (1993) *Managing Autonomous Schools: the Grant Maintained Experience.* London: Paul Chapman.

Carr, W. and Kemmis, S. (1993) 'Action research in education', in Hammersley, M. (Ed) *Controversies in Classroom Research,* 2nd edn. Milton Keynes: Open University Press.

Central Advisory Council for Education (England) (1959) (*Crowther Report 15 to 18*), II, London: HMSO.

Cohen, L. and Manion, L. (1980) *Research Methods in Education.* London: Croom Helm.

Curran, J. (1977) 'Messages and meanings', Unit 6 for OU course, *Mass Communications and Society,* Milton Keynes: Open University Press.

Deming, W.E. (1944) 'On errors in surveys'. *American Sociological Review,* **9,** 359–369.

Denzin, N.K. (1978) *The Research Act,* New York: McGraw-Hill.

Dexter, L.A. (1970) *Elite and Specialized Interviewing.* Evanston: Northwestern University Press.

Evans, K.M. (1984) *Planning Small Scale Research,* 3rd Edn. Windsor: NFER-Nelson.

Fisher, R.A. (1951). *The Design of Experiments,* 6th Edn. Scotland: Oliver and Boyd.

Glaser, B. and Strauss, A. (1967) *The Discovery of Grounded Theory,* London: Weidenfeld and Nicolson.

Gold, R.L. (1969) 'Roles in sociological field observations', in McCall G.S. and Simmons, J.L. (Eds) *Issues in Participant Observation,* Reading, Mass: Addison-Wesley.

Government Statistical Service (1992) *Social Trends 22.* London: HMSO (published annually).

Hammersley, M. and Atkinson, P. (1989) *Ethnography: Principles in Practice.* London: Routledge.

Harris, R. (1986) *Selling Hitler*, London: Faber.

Haywood, P. and Wragg, E.C. (1978) *Rediguide 2: Evaluating the Literature*, School of Education, Nottingham University.

Hilsum, S. and Kane, B.S. (1971) *The Teacher's Day*, Windsor: NFER.

Hinchcliffe, G. (1978) *Piecing Together: the Pedagogical Model*, in Chadwick, A.F., Hind. G., Stevens, M.D. and Tolley, B.H. *Rediguide 15: Historical Research*, School of Education, Nottingham University.

Hinchcliffe, G., Stevens, M.D. and Tolley, B.H. (1978) *Rediguide 15: Historical Research*, School of Education, Nottingham University.

Hoinville, R. and Jowell, R. (1978) *Survey Research Practice*, London: Heinemann.

Howard, K. and Sharp, J.A. (1983) *The Management of a Student Research Project*, Aldershot: Gower.

Johnson, D. (1976) 'Enlisting the participation of teachers in educational research'. *Research Intelligence*, II.

Johnson, D. (1984) 'Planning small-scale research' in Bell et al. (Eds) *Conducting Small-Scale Investigations in Educational Management*, London: Harper and Row.

Johnson, D. (1987) *Private Schools and State Schools: Two Systems or One?*, Milton Keynes: Open University Press.

Johnson, D. (1990) 'Workshop Materials' (unpublished).

Johnson, D. (1993) *Using Documents to Check on Interview Data*. (for *Part II*).

Johnson, D., and Ransom, E. (1983) *Family and School*, London: Croom Helm.

Johnson, M. (1970) *Derbyshire Village Schools*, Newton Abbot: David & Charles.

Kalton, G. (1966) *Introduction to Statistical Ideas for Social Scientists*, London: Chapman and Hall.

Kane, E. (1985) *Doing your own Research*, London: Marion Boyars.

Kogan, M., Johnson, D., Packwood, T. and Whitaker, T. (1984) *School Governing Bodies*, London: Heinemann.

Kogan, M. and Packwood, T. (1974) *Advisory Councils and Committees in Education*, London: Routledge and Kegan Paul.

Miller, S. (1984). *Experimental Design and Statistics*. 2nd Edn. London: Routledge.

Moser, C.A. and Kalton, G. *Survey Methods in Social Investigation*, 2nd Edn. (1971) Aldershot: Gower.

Newson, J., and Newson, E. (1976) 'Parental roles and social contexts' in Shipman, M. (Ed) *The Organisation and Impact of Social Research*, London: Routledge and Kegan Paul.

Nias, J. (1987) 'The primary school staff relationships project: origins, aims and methods'. *Cambridge Journal of Education*, **17**, 2, 83–85.

Nie, N.H. et al. (1975) *Statistical Package for the Social Sciences*, New York: McGraw-Hill.

Nisbet, J. and Watt, J. *Rediguide 26: Case Study. Guides in Educational Research*, School of Education, Nottingham University. (Abridged in Bell, J. et al. (Eds) (1984) *Conducting Small-scale Investigations in Educational Management*, London: Harper and Row.)

Oppenheim, A.N. (1966) *Questionnaire Design and Attitude Measurement*, London: Heinemann.

Popper, K. (1979) *Objective Knowledge* (Revised Edn.) Oxford: Clarendon Press.

Powney, J. and Watts, M. (1987) *Interviewing in Educational Research*, London: Routledge and Kegan Paul.

Richardson, S.A., Dohrenwend, B., Klein, D. (1965), *Interviewing*, New York: Basic Books.

Sammons, P. (1989) 'Ethical issues and statistical work', in Burgess, R.G. (Ed) *The Ethics of Educational Research*, London: Falmer Press.

Scott, C. (1961) 'Research on mail surveys'. *Journal of the Royal Statistical Society*, A, 124, 143–205.

Scott, J. (1990) *A Matter of Record*, Cambridge: Polity Press.

Selltiz, C. et al. (1965) (Revised Edn.) *Research Methods in Social Relations*, London: Methuen.

Silvey, J. (1975) *Deciphering Data*, London: Longman.

Southworth, G. (1987) 'The experience of fieldwork; or insider dealings, who profits?' *Cambridge Journal of Education*, **17**, 2, 86–88.

Stacey, M. (Ed) (1969) *Comparability in Social Research*, London: Heinemann.

Stillman, A. (Ed) (1986) *The Balancing Act of 1980: Parents, Politics and Education*, Slough: NFER.

Stillman, A., and Maychell, K. (1986) *Choosing Schools: Parents, LEAs and the 1980 Education Act*, Windsor: NFER-Nelson.

de Vaus, D.A. (1986) *Surveys in Social Research*, London: Unwin Hyman.

Walker, R. (1985) *Doing Research: a Handbook for Teachers*, London: Methuen.

Webb, E.J., Campbell, D.T., Schwartz, R.D. and Sechrest, L. (1966) *Unobtrusive Measures: Non-Reactive Research in the Social Sciences*, Chicago: Rand McNally.

Whyte, W.F. (1955) *Street Corner Society: the Social Structure of an Italian Slum*, 2nd Edn. Chicago: University of Chicago Press.

Whyte, W.F. (1960) 'Interviewing in field research' in Adams, R. and Preiss, J. (Eds) *Human Organization Research, Field Relations and Techniques*, Homewood, Illinois: Dorsey Press.

Wiles, P. (1971) 'Criminal statistics and sociological explanations of crime' in Carson, W.G. and Wiles, P. (Eds) *Crime and Delinquency in Britain*, Oxford: Martin Robertson.

Williams G.L. (1984) 'Observing and recording meetings' in Bell, J. et al.

Woods, P. (1979) *The Divided School*, London: Routledge and Kegan Paul.

Yeomans, R.Y. (1987) 'Checking and adjusting the lens: case study clearance' *Cambridge Journal of Education*, **17**, 2, 89–90.

Yin, R. (1984) *Case Study Research: Design and Methods.* Beverley Hills: Sage.

Zimmerman, D.H. and Wieder, D.L. (1977) 'The diary — diary-interview method' *Urban Life*, 5, 4, January, 479–498.

Part II

Reading 1

An Introduction to Probability Sampling

Blalock, H. (1970) *An Introduction to Social Research*, New Jersey: Prentice-Hall, Inc. pp. 51–58

❑ Probability sampling

[...] In the case of sample surveys considerable attention is ordinarily given to sampling procedures. These procedures will usually involve what is referred to as a probability sample. The essential feature of a probability sample is that each individual in the entire population, to which a generalization is being made, must have a *known* probability of appearing in the sample. Before considering several kinds of probability sampling procedures, let us discuss in a general way why sampling is so important.

Suppose you have been told on a news report that a survey has been conducted showing that 60 per cent of the Protestants sampled intended to vote Republican, whereas only 40 per cent of the Catholics expected to vote Republican. Of course you might want to know the implications of this fact for the final vote tabulation, in which case it would be necessary to know the proportions of Protestants and Catholics in the area. But let us assume that you are primarily interested in this difference, which amounts to 20 per cent and which seems to require some kind of explanation.

What are the questions you should ask? First, you would wish to know how the sample was selected. Were these simply friends of the announcer, or were they selected 'scientifically'? Another question is: 'How accurate are the responses in terms of the way people will actually vote'? We shall here assume that this particular question can be answered by pointing to previous successes in predicting voting behaviour from such surveys. The specific question I should like to deal with involves the size of the sample. Consider the situations in Tables 1.1, 1.2, 1.3, 1.4, and 1.5.

The figures in the body of each table refer to the actual numbers of people sampled. In Table 1.1 there are only ten people in all, whereas there are two thousand in Table 1.5. In all five tables, however, the percentage of Protestants and Catholics favouring the Republicans are 60 and 40 respectively.

Clearly, one would not have much faith in the generalizability of the results of Table 1.1 and 1.2, containing ten and twenty cases respectively. But what

Table 1.1

	Protestant	Catholic	Total
Republican	3	2	5
Democrat	2	3	5
Total	5	5	10

Table 1.2

	Protestant	Catholic	Total
Republican	6	4	10
Democrat	4	6	10
Total	10	10	20

Table 1.3

	Protestant	Catholic	Total
Republican	30	20	50
Democrat	20	30	50
Total	50	50	100

Table 1.4

	Protestant	Catholic	Total
Republican	60	40	100
Democrat	40	60	100
Total	100	100	200

Table 1.5

	Protestant	Catholic	Total
Republican	600	400	1000
Democrat	400	600	1000
Total	1000	1000	2000

about Table 1.3? Table 1.4? Just what are the chances of finding a 20 per cent difference between Protestants and Catholics in each instance? Intuition would be a very good guide here, although it seems 'obvious' that one should have more faith that a real difference exists within the large population in the case of the last table than in the first. But exactly what is meant by this statement, and how does one go about pinning down the odds?

This is a problem in statistical inference, a relatively complex field based on the mathematical laws of probability. In this simple kind of example the probabilities can be specified if the method of sampling has been a proper one. But if we do not know how the cases were selected, nothing much can be said. If we know that the sample is a 'random' sample (see below), then we may say that if there were in fact no difference in the larger population between the percentages of Protestants and Catholics preferring the Republicans, then the chances are very high that sampling fluctuations alone could account for the results of Tables 1.1 and 1.2. The chances of getting a 20 per cent sample difference in Table 1.3 are about one in twenty (written $P = .05$); for Table 1.4 they are less than one in a hundred ($P < .01$), and for Table 1.5 they are infinitesimal.[1]

It would be nice if we could attain certainty, but unless we collected data on the entire population this result would be impossible. Given the huge size of the voting population, such an aim would obviously be impractical. But we see from these particular examples that there are some general principles that make it possible to give precise probabilities of particular sets of outcomes which, together with any information we might have about measurement accuracy, give us a rational basis for evaluating the confidence we have in the survey results.

One general principle is intuitively obvious. Other things being equal, the larger the sample the more confidence we have that sample results (e.g. a 20 per cent difference) will approximate the true figures for the population. Less obvious is the point that it is the *size* of the sample that counts, not the proportion of the population that it represents. This statement is not quite true if the sample comes almost as large as the population, but it is a very good approximation. If the sample is really a random one, we have just as much faith in the results of the fifth table, regardless of whether the population contains twenty thousand or twenty million persons. This runs counter to the common sense argument people sometimes raise to the effect that surveys can't really be any good because they themselves have never been asked for their opinions. It is in fact possible to get very good estimates of voting intentions from a sample of two thousand, even where one is dealing with the entire population of the United States. Naturally, only a small *proportion* of people would be selected in such a sample.

Another principle that is consistent with common sense is that the bigger the difference found in the sample, the less likely it is that this difference could have occurred purely by chance, other things being equal. In our example we are assuming a 20 per cent difference, but perhaps it might have been 10 per cent or 30 per cent. However, common sense is not very good at telling us whether we should have more faith in a 20 per cent difference with four hundred cases or a 30 per cent difference with two hundred cases. These kinds of questions can only be answered by the statistician.

Finally, the amount of faith we should have in a given size difference for a fixed sample size is also a function of the *kind* of probability sample that has been drawn. Let us therefore consider briefly three kinds of probability samples that are often combined in complex surveys but are at least analytically distinct. In complex sample surveys, where combinations are used, the formula for calculating probabilities can become fairly complex, but fortunately, we do not need to concern ourselves with these matters.

The simplest kind of probability sample conceptually is the 'random' sample. In a random sample all combinations of persons have an equal probability of being selected. This also means that each individual has the same chance of being selected as any other individual. Random samples can be selected by obtaining a complete listing of all population members and then using a table of random numbers or some other random device for selecting them. In practice, this is equivalent to drawing names from a hat, balls from an urn, or cards from a well shuffled deck. But it is a bit more exact, since pieces of paper may stick together, and shuffling is always imperfect.

It is important to recognize that random sampling does not refer to hit-or-miss sampling. One cannot obtain a random sample by interviewing the first hundred people he sees on the street corner or by accepting the first one hundred telephone responses to a radio appeal. Think about the possible biases this kind of sampling can produce. Obviously, the person who never visits the street corner or turns on his radio has no chance of being selected. Remember that we must know the chances of each person's being selected in order to calculate probabilities. We cannot know this without some kind of listing and a random device for pulling names from this list.

A second kind of probability sample is the 'stratified' sample, which also involves a random selected procedure *within* each of several strata or groupings of individuals. The most common reason why we first group individuals and then select a certain number of cases within each grouping is that we may wish to compare the groups, and a purely random sample might not provide enough cases for doing this. If one wanted to compare Jews with Protestants, a straight random sample of two hundred persons might yield only ten Jews selected by chance. As an alternative, one might obtain separate lists of Protestants and Jews (the two strata) and sample one hundred randomly from each list. Obviously, the principles of stratification can be extended to multiple groupings. One might subdivide his population into four strata: white-collar Protestants, white-collar Jews, blue-collar Protestants, and blue-collar Jews, selecting fifty cases from each. There are also some other more subtle advantages of using stratified samples, but this is not the place to discuss them.

It should be recognised that stratified samples will ordinarily not give every individual an equal chance of being selected. In our example, the Jews will be deliberately oversampled, since we wish to obtain enough of them to compare them with the Protestants. That is, each Jew will have a higher probability of being selected than each Protestant. Perhaps the sample will consists of one hundred Protestants from a list of ten thousand and one hundred Jews from a list of two hundred. Then each Protestant has one chance in a hundred of being sample, and each Jew has one chance in two. Since this fact is known, however, and since each Protestant who happens to be sampled represents ninety-nine others, whereas each Jew in the sample represents only one other Jew, the statistician can correct for this known bias by introducing the proper weights in his analysis.

The third type of probability sample is actually the most practical one in large-scale surveys. Lists of American voters simply do not exist. Even city directories get out of date very rapidly, and most counties do not have accurate lists of their residents. (Many lists, such as telephone directories and auto-registration lists, are obviously biased in favour of middle-class and upper-class individuals.) There are, however, lists of counties within the United States or census tracts and blocks within cities. A random sample of such counties or blocks might first be selected. If the resulting geographic area is still very large, the selected areas (e.g. counties) can be subdivided and sub-areas again randomly selected. Finally, a random (or stratified) sample may be selected from within those areas that have been previously selected.

This form of sampling is referred to as 'cluster' or 'area' sampling and is much more complex than the previous two kinds. Its obvious advantage is that it saves the cost of obtaining complete lists. Only those counties or census tracts that have been selected (randomly) need to be subdivided still further. Also, there will be considerable savings on interviewer costs. In a nation-wide sample it would obviously be extremely costly to send trained interviewers all over the country to pick up a few interviews here and there (perhaps five in Montana, three in Nevada, and one in Alaska). But having selected, say, fifty counties at random, and then selected individuals within each of these counties, the investigator can make each interviewer responsible for only one or two counties.

The problem with such cluster samples is that one must avoid extremely homogeneous clusters or areas. A film made several years ago about a so-called typical town in the Mid-west that was found to represent the rest of the country involved a number of humorous episodes when this fact was learned. Needless to say, the town's typicality was soon destroyed. This is an example of the extreme form of a cluster sample (one cluster) that might be ideal from the standpoint of saving interviewing costs. But it depends on the community being heterogeneous enough so that all viewpoints are represented in exactly their proper proportions. Of course we know that no such single communities exist, but perhaps a set of ten or twenty could be found. The opposite extreme would be the community that is perfectly homogeneous, so that any one individual is exactly like the rest. Then we would only need to interview one person to know everything, and even though we interviewed two thousand our effective sample size would be only one! Needless to say, the selection of this kind of community in our sample could give rise to extremely misleading results — either two thousand Republicans or two thousand Democrats.

It does turn out that people who live close together tend to be relatively similar with respect to many of the variables social scientists wish to study: education, income levels, political preferences, or prejudice levels. Yet they are rarely completely homogeneous, Therefore it becomes necessary to juggle the economic advantages of their proximity with the degree to which they are so homogeneous that it would be unwise to interview more than a small number of person from each area. As can be imagined, the problems of selecting an optimum sample become highly complex at this stage and require the experience of experts.

One important general point should be made before leaving the subject of sampling. Once the sample has been selected by sound principles, it becomes essential that a very high percentage of those who have been selected by probability means actually be interviewed and their responses used in the survey. If they may select themselves out of the survey for varying reasons, then the probability nature of the sampling procedure is destroyed. Suppose, for example, that 20 per cent refused to be interviewed and another 20 per cent could not be located because they were not at home at convenient times of the day. Since we would not know very much about these individuals, other than that they refused or were not at home, we could not claim that we knew the probabilities of each type being actually selected (and used) in the survey. All kinds of unknown biases might creep into the study. Some refusals will always occur, and it is the task of methodological studies to determine in a general way the kinds of biases these are likely to introduce. But there is no substitute for a response rate of at least 80 or 90 per cent. This means that interviewers must employ interpersonal skills and be persistent in calling back, perhaps as many as five or six times, in order to locate people who are rarely at home. [...]

❏ Footnote

1. Procedures for computing such probabilities in simple tables of this sort are discussed under the heading of 'chi square' in practically all textbooks on applied statistics. The crucial point is that all such computations require the assumption that a probability sampling procedure has been used and that measurement error is negligible.

 **Reading 2**

Errors of Interpretation in Surveys

Hoinville, R., Jowell, R. et al. (1978) *Survey Research Practice*, London: Heinemann. pp. 183–185

❏ Caveats and conclusions

[...] Faulty interpretations arise partly from the tendency to demand too much of surveys. On the surface, behavioural data, for example, should be easier to interpret than attitudinal data, since most people can describe what they do rather more accurately than they can communicate what their values are. Yet, this is not always so: memory can be faulty, definitions can be ambiguous, answers can be deceptive. Moreover, wrong conclusions can be drawn if insufficient account is taken of the factors governing behaviour and their relationship with the survey purpose. People who have a low tolerance of noise, for instance, will not be found in their true population proportions living near an airport or on a noisy road. A survey of residents around an airport could not therefore be used to describe the noise tolerance levels likely to be found in the rest of the population. Nor could a survey that showed that airport residents were as tolerant of their noise levels as residents of a country village were of theirs be used to conclude that airport noise causes no special annoyance. It would probably mean that the majority of people now exposed to high noise levels consists of those best able to tolerate or adapt to them.

Interpretation becomes still more problematical in surveys that attempt to collect data about intended or future behaviour. Whereas many people can answer with confidence how often say, they play tennis, or when they last played, or when they first took it up, most people are demonstrably bad at predicting how often they would play if more tennis courts were available, or if a new sports complex were built in their area. Their answers, however confident, are little better than guesses. Changes in circumstances or priorities will render their forecasts inaccurate. Moreover, people do not generally possess sufficient knowledge to make reliable forecasts: they cannot know in advance of the event how a new sports complex will affect the use of other local amenities or the extent to which it will release a latent demand for tennis in the area, either of which could change their propensity to use the facility.

In these circumstances researchers sometimes attempt to incorporate an educational element into their surveys. They may, for example, provide respondents with detailed information about the new sports facility and the way in which other facilities have worked in other areas in the hope that the implications will be absorbed quickly enough for respondents to make informed and balanced judgements about their future behaviour. The approach should not be belittled, but it can hardly overcome the inherent weaknesses in asking respondents to forecast their likely behaviour patterns.

There are similar inherent weaknesses in attempting to make forecasts by extrapolating from existing behaviour patterns and characteristics. Detailed information about present behaviour will offer suggestions about the future, but it cannot be used for precise forecasts because it takes no account of which aspects of present behaviour are governed by the facilities available, which by choice, which by habit, which by fashion, and so on.

For all these reasons, surveys should be regarded essentially as a means by which we can document, analyse and interpret past and present attitudes and behaviour patterns. By exposing trends, they will certainly provide clues about the future, but they are only clues.

In attitudinal research also, the primary cause of errors in interpretation is the temptation to read too much into the data or to ignore their shortcomings. A newspaper report that merely quotes an opinion poll finding that, say, 50 per cent of the population support capital punishment or abortion law reform, makes the extraordinary assumption that public opinion is well formed and dichotomous on those issues. The opposite is usually true of most political and social issues. People's views are ambivalent, sometimes because they feel they lack the information or understanding to make proper judgements, sometimes because they cannot decide between the attractions of competing arguments, mostly because they have not been required to consider the issue seriously or to come to any conclusion about it. Given more information, more discussion, more opportunity for reflection and more experience of the alternatives, their conclusion might well differ from their spontaneous reactions. A warning of the limits of interpretation that ought to have been placed on the answers to single opinion questions is provided by Davis (1971, p.20) who observes: 'It is well known that the distributions of answers on attitude and opinion questions will vary by 15 or 20 per cent with apparently slight changes in question wording.'

Any interpretation of survey data that ignores these considerations is bound to be suspect. For this reason comprehensive attitudinal surveys include questions on knowledge and experience so that expressed views can be placed in a wider context and assessed accordingly. They include questions that elicit strength of feeling, which is at least as important as the direction of feeling in relation to an issue. They try to take account of the variation in people's expectations created by their different experiences and different backgrounds: old people, for example, tend to express greater satisfaction with (or is it resignation about?) their living conditions or incomes than young people in similar circumstances do. The researcher also has to interpret attitudinal data in the context of social and environmental conditions that can substantially alter people's outlooks: those who live in very poor housing conditions, for instance, are likely to be so obsessed by their immediate problems as to appear indifferent to more abstract issues. The interpretation of survey data should ideally take all these factors, and others, into account before it can inspire confidence. [...]

 **Reading 3**

Research by Case Study

Kogan, M., Johnson, D., Packwood, T. and Whitaker, T. (1984) *School Governing Bodies*, London: Heinemann. pp.181–184 and 191–192

❏ Appendix 1

❏ Methods of the research

The overall strategy of the research was one of naturalistic enquiry, in Denzin's[1] terms. There was no need to make out artificial boundaries for an area of study, or to set up experimental situations. Governing bodies already existed in which we could explore, in microcosm, the nature of political systems, the exchanges and dependencies between them, the relationship between values and process, theories of representation and participation and the nature of accountability in education. Governing body meetings were the natural and primary focus for our research. Our methodological problems were to ensure that our observations of these and other events accurately, reliably and validly reflected the behaviour recorded, and to decide how, and how far, we should explore around and beyond the corporate life of the governing body to understand its meaning for participants and its political and institutional context. A further problem was the need to assemble, reflect and report on our research material in a way which would be helpful for practitioners and policy-makers in school government, as well as for political scientists.

❏ The case study mode

Given the resources available for the study — a small team of researchers able to work full-time on the project over a period of three years — and the apparently episodic corporate life of the phenomena to be studied (governing bodies), the case study mode was an obvious choice. Case study work (rather than, for example, a survey method which might entail the employment of hired interviewers) would make good use of the resources of people and time already available for the research. Extended case study work enables the dynamic of institutional processes, and individual relationships, to be monitored and appraised over time. Moreover, case studies provide a data base for analytic description of components and processes and for model-building, and these were among the objectives of our research.

❑ Comparability of the case studies

The case study method has as one of its strengths the ability to explore diversity of practice. Nevertheless, if several such studies are carried out as part of a single project, some comparable elements should form part of each case examined. In the school governing bodies project the same range of techniques was employed in each study — observations, semi-structured interviews, and the study of documents. Coverage, in terms of interviews undertaken, was founded on two principles: the notion of reputational sampling (i.e. making contact with those who are seen to be important to other people) and the more systematic coverage of a range of incumbents of formal roles which, although not necessarily seen to be important reputationally, plainly had legitimacy and relevance in our study area.

The first stage in each case study was the general examination of current educational and political issues in the LEA, through the study of documents. Field work with the particular governing body usually began with the observation of a governing body meeting, together with the study of minutes of earlier meetings. Interviews then ensued with the chairman, all or most of the governors, the headteacher, and other staff at the school, using the 'reputational' and 'systematic' criteria described above. Where relevant, school meetings were observed and documents examined, to identify points of organisational change, development and/or stability, and to monitor the emergence of demands which might or might not impact on governing bodies, also the reactions of teachers to any governing body initiatives. All governing body meetings, whether regular or specially convened, were observed over a period of four school terms. During the same period, some parents were interviewed to explore the practice as well as the rhetoric of home/school relations. Beyond the immediate orbit of the schools, local educational issues were monitored through a study of the local press and attendance at public meetings. Where appropriate, meetings of educational interest groups were attended and interviews undertaken. At the level of the local authorities, key councillors and officers were interviewed, some non-public working parties and sub-committees observed, and other regular meetings monitored through the study of documents. Repeated interviews were held with key governors (in particular the chairman and the headteacher or deputy headteacher) and any changes in governing body membership were followed up.

Particular educational or political issues which happened to become a focus of interest during the period of case study were followed through, in school and/or locality, and provided an opportunity to study interaction between school, governing body and community. Examples of these were the expansion of a school's sphere of operation to include community education, and a proposal to establish tertiary colleges in one of the authorities.

❏ Validity of the data base

In this project, the problems of validity in the case study mode were tackled at a number of levels. Cross-checking took place through the use of differing research techniques (interview, observation, study of documents). Validity was also tested through team discussion, when the accumulated knowledge of the individual researcher about his research 'patch' was explored and criticised. At the end of each case study, a written account of acquired information was submitted for confirmation to the chairman of the governing body, the headteacher and senior figures in the local authority. Towards the end of the project reflective analysis was tested in seminar groups of research participants and practitioners in the field of study.

❏ Selection of LEAs and governing bodies for case study

Consideration of the criteria to be applied in selecting local education authorities and governing bodies passed through several stages, some of them proceeding the funded period of the research.

Eventually it was decided to make a judgement sample based chiefly on four criteria: type of local education authority, political culture of the local authority, type of school and governing body composition.

Once the criteria for selection are established it is relatively simply to identify suitable authorities and institutions. Research access can never be taken for granted, and must always be carefully negotiated, but it is equally important not to request access and then fail to follow through with research because of a change in criteria. No insoluble problems with regard to access were encountered in the authorities eventually approached. The sample of eight case studies chosen had the following features:

Type of local education authority:	1 shire county
	1 large metropolitan
	2 outer urban
Political culture of local authority:	2 Labour, 2 Conservative (1980–2)
Type of school(s) governed:	*age range*
	Infants & Juniors 5–11
	J, M & I voluntary aided 5–11

First & Middle	5–12
High	12–16
Secondary	11–18 (n=3)
Special (ESN M&S)	11–16

Governing body composition: 6 individual governing bodies
2 joint governing bodies
(pattern and balance of membership was varied)

The selection of the actual schools and governing bodies to be approached was influenced by local authority suggestions and guidance, but in all cases research access was personally negotiated with the headteachers and chairman of governors concerned. [...]

❑ Scope and manner of the fieldwork
In all, 369 interviews were carried out, and 51 full meetings of the case study governing bodes were observed; 52 other meetings or events were also observed. These included sub-committee meetings of governors, LEA working parties, parents' meetings and staff meetings in the schools, and various other school events, as well as training meetings for governors and meetings of local groups.

❑ Governing body meetings and other observation sessions
Researchers received the same agenda papers as governors. They did not contribute to the meetings, unless asked to report on the progress of the research. Following each meeting, a typewritten analysis of what took place was circulated for internal discussion by the research team. These analyses were prepared from notes.

All other meetings observed, including staff appointment meetings, were similarly written up.

❑ Interviews
These were recorded in note form by the researcher concerned, and typed up for team study. Interviews lasted from 40 minutes to $2^1/_2$ hours. Most interviews were single events, but some key informants were seen 4 to 6 times.

A very flexible approach was taken to the task of interviewing governors. Interviews were arranged at whatever time and place was convenient for them. In a handful of cases, when it proved impossible for a governor or other respondent to see the researcher, telephone interviews were conducted. A few interviews of this kind were also carried out when exploring the ramifications of interest groups in the community. The particular problems of mapping community links with schools and governing bodies are further discussed below.

Before embarking on any of the field work, guidelines for the interviews with the main role-holders (headteachers, governing body chairman, education committee chairman, education officers) were jointly worked out by the research team. A checklist was also prepared of the items to be covered in the case study as a whole.

❑ Study of documents

In each LEA a special study was made of local Instruments and Articles of Government, as amended over a period of 10–15 years, and of any Hand-books or Guideline Notes supplied to governors. Minutes of the Education Committee and/or schools sub-committee spanning a three-year period were studied. Where appropriate, internal education department documents, joint consultative committee and Diocesan Board papers were also studied. Local newspapers were monitored throughout the research period for relevant issues in the local authority.

For each of the case-study governing bodies, the minutes of meetings over several years prior to the research were examined, together with headteachers' reports to the governing body over the period, where available. Papers submitted to the governing body by other members of staff were also studied, together with certain internal school documents such as staff bulletins and minutes of staff meetings. Where appropriate, PTA and PTFA documentation was examined, and information provided to parents by the school was monitored over the research period. This included brochures and material circulated by pupil post, including parent governors election papers. Papers relating to certain local groups were also studied.

❑ Exploring community links with education

This was the least cut-and-dried area of the field work, and a number of techniques were used to establish which sections of the community had special educational interests to promote, and what channels they attempted to use.

Depending on the character of the area, researchers severally:

- made a broad scan of local interests by examining locally available lists of organisations and groups

- drew on previous research experience and used local knowledge to make contacts with particular networks of interest
- identified key informants from the study of documents or by a 'snowballing' system of interviews
- followed up publicity material displayed in schools or local libraries, also news items in local papers
- interviewed individuals, in person or by telephone, entered into correspondence and/or attended meetings

all with a view to ascertaining what interest groups existed, what aspects of education they were concerned to influence, if any, what knowledge they had of school governing bodies and whether in particular instances they made representations to governing body, school or LEA. [...]

❏ Reference

1. Denzin, N.K. (1978) *The Research Act*, London: McGraw-Hill

 **Reading 4**

Social Research and Documentary Sources

Scott, J. (1990) *A Matter of Record*, Cambridge: Polity Press

Figure 4.1 A classification of documents

		Authorship		
		Personal	Official	
			Private	State
Access	Closed	1	5	9
	Restricted	2	6	10
	Open-archival	3	7	11
	Open-published	4	8	12

[...] The dimension of authorship refers to the origin of the documents, and its applicability is clearly dependent upon the existence of a separation between the 'personal' and the 'public' or 'official' spheres and, within the latter, between the State and private bureaucracies. The distinction between the personal and the official world was central to Weber's discussion of the rise of modern bureaucratic administration, with its separation of the 'household' from the 'office'. This differentiation is a hallmark of the modern period and the classification in Figure 1 has less relevance to the medieval and earlier periods, when the distinction between 'personal' papers, 'Church' papers and 'State' papers was not made at all sharply — if, indeed, it was made at all; and it is only in recent history that official prime ministerial documents in Britain, for example, have ceased to be regarded as the personal property of the Prime Minister.

The dimension of 'access' refers to the availability of the documents to people other than their authors. Documents subject to 'closed' access are those which are available only to a limited circle of eligible insiders, normally to those who produce them and to their bureaucratic superiors. By contrast, 'restricted' documents are accessible on an *ad hoc* basis under specified conditions to those outsiders who are able to secure the permission of insiders; they are therefore, normally closed to outsider access, though their authors or custodians may be willing to grant access on application. 'Archival' access exists where the documents have been lodged in a place of storage which is open to all comers; researchers and the general public therefore may use an archive subject only to minimal administrative restrictions — such as the need to apply for a reader's ticket, supply references, and attend during opening hours — and can consult all documents lodged in that archive. Finally, 'published' documents are the most 'open' of all, in the sense that they are printed for public circulation, generally on a commercial basis, and so are accessible to all who can afford them or can obtain them in a library. (As will be seen, however, the fact that particular documents may be openly published does not mean that they are any less difficult to interpret: openness of access is not at all the same thing as openness of meaning!).

Personal documents which are subject to closed access, type 1 in Figure 1, are perhaps very familiar from the letters, diaries, household account books, address books, and domestic ephemera which are kept by many people. Diaries, for example, are normally completely 'closed' documents — accessible only to the individual author — unless they take the form of an appointment book, when a wider family circle or a secretary may have routine access. But a diary may sometimes be written with the self-conscious intent of informing a wider public through eventual publication, as a diary or in the form of a memoir or autobiography. In such circumstances the diary becomes a document of type 4. As will be show in a later chapter, however, the closed and the open diary are often of a very different character and require different handling, as the intention to publish may have coloured the author's style and attitude. Even the discovery and publication of a closed diary by a third party involves critical problems of interpretation. Besides the published diary are other published personal documents such as novels, plays, poems and non-fiction works (biographies and scientific works, for example), as well as such things a 'letters to the editor' in a newspaper, and printed sermons and speeches. What unites all these varieties of documents is authorship outside the public sphere and the fact of publication.

Some personal documents (type 3), mainly those of wealthy and well-known families, have been deposited in archives, libraries and record offices, and this makes it more possible for the researcher to study them than if they had remained in private hands. The records of many landed estates and lords of the manor, for example, were produced before the distinction between the personal and the official was institutionalised, and remained as part of the day-to-day documentation of the household. In many cases such documents remain still in private ownership and are, therefore, closed to public access unless the owners are able to establish a private archive in their own house and grant restricted access to the archived documents (type 2). There is thus a progression from the completely closed personal documents to the completely open. Some may move from one category to another over the course of their lifetimes: the household accounts of a wealthy landowner, for example, may be 'closed' when in current use, but may eventually pass into the hands of a public archive; and if a researcher 'discovers' a document in an archive and regards it as important source material it may be commercially published and thus become more readily available to other researchers.

Official documents in the private sphere — produced by businesses, schools, hospitals, the church, and so on — may also range from the closed to the open. Typical of private closed documents (type 5) are confidential records and reports produced in organisations and which remain in current use: medical records of the treatment given to patients by their doctors and in hospitals, for example, are normally accessible only to those with responsibility for the patients. Some private organisations have records falling under each of the four categories of access. For instance, businesses registered under the American Securities Exchange Act and quoted on the Stock Exchange have to publish annual reports and accounts (documents of type 8), but the current records of sales, wages, etc., which are contained in their ledgers, minute books and memos, and which are used to compile the published accounts, are normally accessible only to the company's managerial and accounting staff (type 5 documents). A requirement of the British Companies Act has been the public disclosure of certain documents for storage in the Companies Registration Office, a massive government archive for business documents of type 7: copies of annual reports and supporting documents such as registers of shareholders and lists of mortgages. Business documents normally subject to closed access may become available to researchers, such as business historians, when they are no longer of current operating relevance; when, as is usually the case, they remain in the company's own offices, they are restricted documents of type 6, but if they have been deposited in public archives (as in the case of some old or defunct companies) they are in the 'open' category, type 7.

Published documents of private origin (type 8) are particularly widespread in libraries and constitute a major source of research material. Typical of such documents are the timetables and directories produced by many commercial and professional organisations on an annual or more frequent basis, but the category also includes pamphlets, newspapers, and other products of the mass media.

Documents produced by governmental authorities, both national and local, comprise the single largest class of documents available to the social researcher, many more being closed to research access. Police records and security reports, local authority housing records, current taxation records and so on are accessible only by those actually involved in their production and official assessment. In Britain such documents (type 9) are generally protected by the Official Secrets Act, which forbids the unauthorised disclosure of anything learnt by a servant of the State in the course of his or her work. Disclosure is generally not authorised for documents which are deemed to have defence or security implications or to contain information which the Government and its senior civil servants wish to keep private. The operation of official secrecy is such that official documents are either closed or open; relatively few are in the intermediate 'restricted' category (type 10); to which access is granted only with permission of the monarch.

Archival access (type 11) is very common for those governmental papers which are classified as 'open', though the vast majority never reach this stage. Examples of archived state documents are the vast range of papers stored in the Public Record Office in Britain or the Library of Congress in the United States. Such documents are available to anyone applying for a reader's ticket and include military and diplomatic dispatches, cabinet minutes, presidential papers, official correspondence and case files, census returns, army and navy records, revenue and taxation records, and so on. In addition to the national record offices, there are various specialist archives which store official documents of type 11 and with varying levels of access. the General Register Office in Britain, for example, maintains an archive of birth, marriage and death registers, the index to which is open to the public who may also purchase certified copies of register entries identified from the index. The registers themselves, however, are closed to all except GRO staff.

The final category of Stage document (type 12) encompasses a huge range of British official publications: reports of Royal Commissions, the Hansard record of parliamentary debates, Acts of Parliament, Census Reports, and an array of statistical publications such as *Social Trends*, and the *Annual Abstract of Statistics*. [...]

 **Reading 5**

Action Research

Cohen, L. and Manion, L. (1980) *Research Methods in Education,* London: Croom Helm

❑ Introduction

We come now to a style of research that has received rather more publicity over the years than most other methods in the social sciences. This may indeed stem from the implied tension in its name, *action research,* for *action* and *research* as separate activities in whatever context each have their own ideology and modus operandi and when conjoined in this way, lie as uneasy bedfellows. To give a comprehensive definition of the term at this stage is difficult because usage varies with time, place and setting. None the less, we may offer a conventional definition and use this as a starting point: *action research is small-scale intervention in the functioning of the real world and a close examination of the effects of such intervention.*[1] By looking at a few examples of the use of the method in the research literature, we may further identify other tangible features: action research is *situational* — it is concerned with diagnosing a problem in a specific context and attempting to solve it in that context; it is usually (though not inevitably) *collaborative* — teams of researchers and practitioners work together on a project; it is *participatory* — team members themselves take part directly or indirectly in implementing the research; and it is *self-evaluative* — modifications are continuously evaluated within the on-going situation, the ultimate objective being to improve practice in some way or other. According to Blum[2], the use of action research in the social sciences can be resolved into two stages: a *diagnostic stage* in which the problems are analysed and the hypotheses developed; and a *therapeutic stage* in which the hypotheses are tested by a consciously directed change experiment, preferably in a social life situation.

The scope of action research as a method is impressive. Its usage may range at one extreme from a teacher trying out a novel way of teaching social studies with his class to, at another, a sophisticated study of organisational change in industry using a large research team and backed by government sponsors. Whatever the situation, however, the method's evaluative frame of reference remains the same, namely, to add to the practitioner's *functional knowledge* of the phenomena he deals with. This type of research is therefore usually considered in conjunction with social or educational aims.[3]

It will be useful here if we distinguish *action research* from *applied research*, for although they are similar in some ways, there are important differences between them which need to be made explicit, for confusion between the two does sometimes arise. Both utilise the scientific method. Since applied research is concerned mainly with establishing relationships and testing theories, it is quite rigourous in its application of the conditions of this method. To this end, therefore, it insists on: studying a large number of cases; establishing as much control as possible over variables; precise sampling techniques; and a serious concern to generalise its findings to comparable situations. It does not claim to contribute directly to the solution of problems. Action research, by contrast, interprets the scientific method much more loosely, chiefly because its focus is a specific problem in a specific setting. The emphasis is not so much on obtaining generalisable scientific knowledge as on precise knowledge for a particular situation and purpose. The conditions imposed on applied research, therefore, are normally relaxed with action research. Of course, as action research projects become more extensive in their coverage, the boundary between the two methods becomes less easy to define. A curriculum project involving 100 schools, say, or a community action programme embracing a number of major conurbations, will tend to yield rather more generalisable knowledge and information than purely localised undertakings.

Having drawn this distinction between action research and applied research, we are now free to concentrate on the former and ask ourselves the question: what kinds of intervention programmes are featured in action research? The following examples, while by no means exhaustive, give some idea of the contexts in which the method may be used. They are not mutually exclusive so there may be considerable overlap between some of them. There is the kind: (1) which acts as a *spur to action*, its objective being to get something done more expeditiously than would be the case with alternative means; (2) which addresses itself to *personal functioning, human relations and morality* and is thus concerned with people's job efficiency, their motivations, relationships and general well-being; (3) which focuses on *job analysis* and aims at improving professional functioning and efficiency; (4) which is concerned with organisational change in so far as it results in improved functioning in business or industry; (5) which is concerned with *planning and policy-making*, generally in the field of social administration; (6) which is concerned with *innovation and change* and the ways in which these may be implemented in on-going systems; (7) which concentrates on *problem-solving* virtually in any context in which a specific problem needs solving; and (8) which provides the opportunity to develop theoretical knowledge, the emphasis here being more on the research element of the method.

Equally diverse are the situations in which these different kinds of intervention may be used — almost any setting, in fact, where a problem involving people, tasks and procedures cries out for a solution, or where some change of feature results in a more desirable outcome. Notable instances of the use of action research may be found in such starkly contrasting worlds as insurance, prisons, social administration, ships, hospitals, community projects, education, industry, coal-mining and business management. Examination of the work of the Tavistock Institute of Human Relations which has done so much to develop action research as a methodology will illustrate how the method may be applied to these diverse areas.[4] For our own purposes, however, we shall now restrict our discussion chiefly to the use of action research in the field of education.

Although the action research movement in education was initiated in the United States in the 1940s, the scene for its appearance began to be set in that country in the 1920s with the application of the scientific method to the study of educational problems, growing interest in group interaction and group processes, and the emerging progressive movement. Indeed, the latter is seen by some as the principal causal agent for subsequent developments in action research. One writer[5] says: 'Action research ... is a direct and logical outcome of the progressive position. After showing children how to work together to solve their problems, the next step was for teachers to adopt the methods they had been teaching their children, and learn to solve their own problems co-operatively'. Reaching its peak in the 1960s, the movement had multifarious aims of a decidedly practical nature which were often embellished with ideological, even political, counterpoints. Some, for instance, saw it as a necessary corrective to the failure of official bodies to implement traditional research findings: others, as a means of improving the quality of life. Action research in Britain has enjoyed something of a revival since the establishment of the Schools Council in 1964 under whose aegis it has been used to implement curriculum research and development. The purpose of action research in school and classroom fall broadly into five categories: (1) it is a means of remedying problems diagnosed in specific situations, or of improving in some way a given set of circumstances; (2) it is a means of in-service training, thereby equipping the teacher with new skills and methods, sharpening his analytical powers and heightening his self-awareness; (3) it is a means of injecting additional or innovatory approaches to teaching and learning into an on-going system which normally inhibits innovation and change; (4) it is a means of improving the normally poor communications between the practising teacher and the academic researcher, and of remedying the failure of traditional research to give clear prescription; and (5) although lacking the rigour of true scientific research, it is a means of providing a preferable alternative to the more subjective, impressionistic approach to problem-solving in the classroom.

Figure 5.1

Humanities curriculum project — aim and premisses

Aim:
To develop an understanding of social situations and human acts and of the controversial value issues which they raise.

Premisses:

1. That controversial issues should be handled in the classroom.

2. That the teacher should accept the need to submit his teaching in controversial areas to the criterion of neutrality at this stage of education, ie that he should regard it as part of his responsibility not to promote his own view.

3. That the mode of enquiry in controversial areas should have discussion, rather than instruction, as its core.

4. That the discussion should protect divergence of view among participants, rather than attempt to achieve consensus.

5. That the teacher as chairman of the discussion should have responsibility for quality and standards of learning.

Source: Butcher and Pont[6]

We close our introduction by asking: who actually undertakes action research in schools? Three possibilities present themselves. First, there is a single teacher operating on his own with his class. He will feel the need for some kind of change or improvement in teaching, learning or organisation, for example, and will be in a position to translate his ideas into action in his own classroom. He is, as it were, both practitioner and researcher in one and will integrate the practical and theoretical orientations within himself. Second, action research may be pursued by a group of teachers working co-operatively within one school, though of necessity functioning against a bigger backdrop than the teacher working solo. They may or may not be advised by an outside teacher. And third, there is the occasion — perhaps the characteristic in recent years — where a team of teachers working alongside a team of researchers in a sustained relationship, possibly with other interested parties, like advisers, university departments and sponsors, on the periphery. This third possibility, though potentially the most promising, may also be the most problematic, at least initially, because of rival characterisations of action and research by the teachers and researchers respectively. We shall return to this point at the end of the chapter. Advocates of action research believe that little can be achieved if only one person is involved in changing his ideas and practices. For this reason, co-operative research tends to be emphasised and encouraged. One commentator[7] notes:

> Action research functions best when it is co-operative action research. This method of research incorporates the ideas and expectations of all persons involved in the situation. Co-operative action research has the concomitant of beneficial effects for workers and the improvement of the services, conditions, and functions of the situation. In education this activity translates into more practice in research and problem-solving by teachers, administrators, pupils, and certain community personnel, while the quality of teaching and learning is in the process of being improved.

❏ Characteristics

The principal characteristics of action research which we hereupon describe are more or less present in all instances of its usage (those having an experimental slant need to be considered in a somewhat different category). We have already referred to its prime feature — that it is essentially an on-the-spot procedure designed to deal with a concrete problem located in an immediate situation. This means that the step-by-step process is constantly monitored (ideally, that is) over varying periods of time and by a variety of mechanisms (questionnaires, diaries, interviews and case studies, for example) so that the ensuing feedback may be translated into modifications, adjustments, directional changes, re-definitions, as necessary, so as to bring about lasting benefit to the on-going process itself rather than to some future occasion, as is the purpose of more traditionally oriented research. Unlike other methods, no attempt is made to identify one particular factor and study it in isolation, divorced from the context giving it meaning. That the findings are applied immediately, then, or in the short term is another important characteristic, although having made this point we need to qualify it to the extent that members of research teams — especially in curriculum projects — frequently have a more long-term perspective. The following extract from Stenhouse's[8] account of the Humanities Curriculum Project illustrates how some of the points we have just made appear 'in the field':

> During the session 1968–9 the schools worked on collections on war, education, and the family. Feedback on materials was by questionnaire supported by interviews with the schools officer or other team members when they visited schools. Information was sought on coverage of the collection, accessibility of the material to the students (readability and sophistication of ideas), and the extent to which materials provoked or

supported discussion. Most schools used only a small proportion of materials (as was intended) so that feedback on any one piece was not extensive. It was also frequently contradictory, particularly as to readability. Collections were radically re-edited as a result of experience in schools; often only half the trial pack survived.

The principal justification for the use of action research in the context of the school is improvement of practice. This can be achieved only if teachers are able to change their attitudes and behaviour. One of the best means of bringing about these kinds of changes is pressure from the group with which one works. As we have seen, because the problems of teachers are often shared with other teachers in the same school, action research has tended to become co-operative involving many or all of the teachers in the school. Group interaction is frequently another characteristic, therefore.

A feature which makes action research a very suitable procedure for work in classrooms and schools (as well as other field settings) is its flexibility and adaptability. These qualities are revealed in the changes that may take place during its implementation and in the course of on-the-spot experimentation and innovation characterising the approach. They come out particularly strongly when set against the usual background of constraints in schools — those to do with organisation, resources, timetabling, staff deployment and teacher's attitudes, for example, as well as pressures from other agencies involved and from competing interests.

Figure 5.2

The ideal teacher for an integrated studies project

The ideal teacher for an Integrated Studies Project would be one willing to maintain his subject discipline within a team and to engage in planning integrated work through discussions with other specialist colleagues. This teacher would be an active producer of new materials, teaching methods and ideas for integrated subject work. He would keep accounts of his innovatory work, fill in the questionnaires sent him by the project team and feed his experience back to them. He would organize his work so that children would not only come to see and use the concepts within separate subject disciplines, but would learn the skills of those subjects through enquiry-based programmes.

Source: Adapted from Shipman [9]

Action research relies chiefly on observation and behaviour data. That it is therefore empirical is another distinguishing feature of the method. This implies that over the period of a project information is collected, shared, discussed, recorded in some way, evaluated and acted upon; and that from time to time, this sequence of events forms the basis of reviews of progress. In this one respect at least it is superior to the more usual subjective, impressionistic methods we have already alluded to. Where an experimental note is introduced into a project, it is generally achieved through the use of control groups with a view to testing specific hypotheses and arriving at more generalisable knowledge.

In our early comparison with applied research, we said that action research took a much more relaxed view of the scientific method. We return to this point here because it is a characteristic which forms the basis of persistent criticisms of the method by its opponents. Travers[10], for example, in reviewing a number of action research projects writes:

> The writer's evaluation of the last fifty studies which have been undertaken which compare the outcomes of one teaching methodology with another is that they have contributed almost nothing to our knowledge of the factors that influence the learning process in the classroom. Many of them do not even identify what the experimentally controlled variables are and indicate only that the study compares the outcomes of educational practices in the community where the study originates with educational practices elsewhere.

That the method should be lacking in scientific rigour, however, is not surprising since the very factors which make it distinctively what it is — and therefore of value in certain contexts — are the antithesis of true experimental research. The points usually made are: that its objective is situational and specific (unlike the scientific method which goes beyond the solution of practical problems); its sample is restricted and unrepresentative; it has little or no control over independent variables; and its findings are not generalisable but generally restricted to the environment in which the research is carried out. While these criticisms hold in most cases, it is important that we refer again to the qualification made earlier: that as action research programmes become more extensive and use more schools, that is, become more standardised, less personalised and more 'open', some of these strictures at least will become less valid.

❑ Occasions when action research as a method is appropriate

We come now to a brief consideration of the occasions when the use of action research is fitting and appropriate. The answer in short is this: that action research is appropriate whenever specific knowledge is required for a specific problem in a specific situation; or when a new approach is to be grafted on to an existing system. More than this, however, suitable mechanisms must be available for monitoring progress and for translating feedback into the on-going system. This means that, other things being equal, the action research method may be applied to any classroom or school situation where these conditions apply. We have already referred to the suitability of the approach to curriculum research and development. Let us now take this further by identifying other areas in school life where action research could be used and illustrate each area with a concrete example: (1) *teaching methods* — perhaps replacing a traditional method by a discovery method; (2) *learning strategies* — adopting an integrated approach to learning in preference to a single subject style of teaching and learning; (3) *evaluative procedures* — improving one's methods of continuous assessment, say; (4) the realm of *attitudes and values* — possibly encouraging more positive attitudes of work, for instance, or modifying pupils' value systems with regard to some aspect of life: (5) the personal *in-service development* of teachers — improving teaching skills, developing new methods of learning, increasing powers of analysis, or heightening self-awareness, for example; (6) *management and control* — the gradual introduction of the techniques of behaviour modification; and (7) *administration* — increasing the efficiency of some aspect of the administrative side of school life.

Of course, it would be naive of us simply to select a problem area *in vacuo*, so to speak. We have also to consider the context in which the project is to be undertaken. More specifically this means bearing in mind factors that will directly affect the outcomes. One of these concerns the teachers themselves and the extent to which they are favourably disposed toward the project, particularly when they are part of a collectivity working with outside agencies for, as we shall see in our final section, this very factor on its own can be a source of intense friction. It is important, therefore, that the teachers taking part in the project are truly involved, that they know what the objectives are, what these imply, and that they are adequately motivated — or a least sufficiently open-minded for motivation to be induced. Another important factor concerns the organisational aspect of the school so that there is a reasonable amount of congruence between the setting and the programme to be initiated. This can be achieved without too much discord when a programme is internally organised by the school itself. When outside parties are involved, however, who themselves are working concurrently in other schools, difficulties may arise over such matters as implementing a new style of teaching, for example, or use of project materials, and so on. One further factor concerns resources: are there enough sufficiently competent researchers at hand? And has the school got reasonable access to college and university libraries to consult appropriate professional and research journals should this need arise? Some or all of these factors need to be reviewed as part of the planning stage of an action research programme.

Figure 5.3

Metaphors reflecting teachers' perceptions of a curriculum project

1. *The exchange of gifts:* the project as reciprocal obligation.

2. *The other drummer:* the project as unselected affinity.

3. *Troubled waters:* the project as agitation or distress.

4. *The gift of grace:* the project as salvation.

5. *New props for identity:* the project as theatre.

6. *Free sample:* the project as commercialism.

7. *Ground bait:* the project as exploitation.

8. *Taking issue:* the project as management consultancy.

9. *Cargo cult:* the project as overwhelming technology.

Source: Shipman[9]

❑ Some issues

We have already seen that the participants in a change situation may be either a teacher, a group of teachers working internally, or else teachers and researchers working on a collaborative basis. It is this latter category, where action research brings together two professional bodies each with its own objectives and values, that we shall consider further at this point because of its inherent problematic nature. Both parties share the same interest in an educational problem, yet their respective orientations to it differ. It has been observed[1], for instance, that research values *precision, control, replications* and attempts to generalise from specific events. Teaching, on the other hand, is concerned with *action, with doing things,* this translates generalisations into specific acts. The incompatibility between action and research in these respects, therefore, can be a source of problems. Marris and Rein[11], for example, on reviewing the relationship between the two in a number of

American community action programmes concluded that the principles of *action* and *experienced research* are so different and so often mutually exclusive that attempts to link them into a single process are likely to produce internal conflict and the subordination of one element to another. They express it thus:

> Research requires a clear and constant purpose, which both defines and proceeds the choice of means; that the means be exactly and consistently followed; and that no revision takes place until the sequence of steps is completed. Action is tentative, non-committal and adaptive. It concentrates upon the next step, breaking the sequence into discrete, manageable decisions. It casts events in a fundamentally different perspective, evolving the future out of present opportunities, where research perceives the present in the context of the final outcomes. Research cannot interpret the present until it knows the answers to its ultimate questions. Action cannot foresee what questions to ask until it has interpreted the present. Action attempts to comprehend all the factors relevant to an immediate problem whose nature continually changes as events proceed, where research abstracts one or two factors for attention, and holds to a constant definition of the problem until the experiment is concluded.

Those who are not quite as pessimistic about the viability of the action/ research coupling would question whether the characterisation of action and research as put forward by Marris and Rein necessarily holds in all contexts. They would advocate a more flexible approach to the relationship. Some researchers[1], for instance, suggest that projects could vary along a number of dimensions such as the degree of control exercised by the action and research components, the amount of knowledge about the means of achieving the desired outcomes, and the level of co-operation between action and research. Such a classification could be linked to different kinds of action research (see p. 175) and suggest what combinations of action and research were most appropriate for particular conditions. In short, what seems to be needed is a clear and unambiguous statement of the project's objectives such that all participants understand them and their implications; and a careful analysis of the context(s) in which the programme is to be mounted to determine the precise, but flexible, relationship between the two components. This would help to ensure that the positive contributions of both are maximised and that the constraints of each on the other are kept to a minimum.

❏ Procedures

We now trace the possible stages and procedures that may be followed in an action research programme, or from which a suitable selection may be made. As we have already seen, projects may vary along a number of dimensions — whether they are to be conducted by teachers only, or by teachers in collaboration with researchers, whether small or large samples of schools are involved, whether they tackle specific problems or more diffuse ones, for example. Given the particular set of circumstances, an appropriate model may be selected to guide procedures, one that will be tailor-make to meet the needs of the change situation in question. As we are here concerned with a review of procedures in general terms, however, and not with a specific instance, we offer a basic, flexible framework by way of illustration: it will need to be interpreted or adjusted in the light of the particular undertaking.

The *first stage* will involve the identification, evaluation and formulation of the problem perceived as critical in an everyday teacher situation. 'Problem' should be interpreted loosely here so that it could refer to the need to introduce innovation into some aspect of a school's established programme. The *second stage* involves preliminary discussion and negotiations among the interested parties — teachers, researchers, advisers, sponsors, possibly — which may culminate in a draft proposal. This may include a statement of the questions to be answered (e.g. Under what conditions can curriculum change be best effected? What are the limiting factors in bringing about effective curriculum change? What strong points of action research can be employed to bring about curriculum change?). The researchers in their capacity as consultants (or sometimes as programme initiators) may draw upon their expertise to bring the problem more into focus, possibly determining causal factors or recommending alternative lines of approach to established ones. This is often the crucial stage for the venture as it is at this point that the seeds of success or failure are planted, for unless the objectives, purposes and assumptions are made perfectly clear to all concerned, and unless the role of key concepts is stressed (e.g. feedback), the enterprise can easily miscarry. The *third stage* may in some circumstances involve a review of the research literature to find out what can be learned from comparable studies, their objectives, procedures, and problems encountered. The *fourth stage* may involve a modification or redeliniation of the initial statement of the problem at stage one. It may now emerge in the form of a testable hypothesis; or as a set of guiding objectives. In Figure 5.1 we give an example of an aim and accompanying premises which were used in this connection in the Humanities Curriculum Project. Sometimes change agents deliberately decide against the use of objectives on the grounds that they have a constraining effect on the process itself. It is also at this stage that assumptions underlying the project are made explicit (e.g. in order to effect curriculum changes, the attitudes, values, skills and objectives of the teachers involved must be changed). The *fifth stage* may be concerned with the selection of research procedures — sampling, administration, choice of materials, methods of teaching and learning, allocation of resources and tasks, deployment of staff and so on.

The *sixth stage* will be concerned with the choice of the evaluation procedures to be used and will need to take into consideration that evaluation in this context will be continuous. Figure 5.4 provides a set of evaluation objectives from the Humanities Project by way of example. The *seventh stage* embraces the implementation of the project itself (over varying periods of time). It will include the conditions and methods of data collection (e.g. biweekly meetings, the keeping of records, interim reports, final reports, the submission of self-evaluation and group-evaluation reports, etc.); the monitoring of tasks and the transmission of feedback to the research team; and the classification and analysis of data. The *eighth and final stage* will involve the interpretation of the data; inferences to be drawn; and overall evaluation of the project. Discussions on the findings will take place in the light of previously agreed evaluative criteria. Errors, mistakes and problems will be considered. A general summing up may follow this in which the outcomes of the project are reviewed, recommendations made, and arrangement for dissemination of results to interested parties decided.

Figure 5.4

The objectives of the evaluation unit in the humanities curriculum project

1. To ascertain the effects of the Project, document the circumstances in which they occur, and present this information in a form which will help educational decision-makers to evaluate the likely consequences of adopting the programme.

2. To describe the present situation and operations of the schools we study so that decision-makers can understand more fully what it is they are trying to change.

3. To describe the work of the project team in terms which will help the sponsors and planners of such a venture to weigh the value of this form of investment, and to determine more precisely the framework of support, guidance and control which are appropriate.

4. To make a contribution to evaluation theory by articulating our problems clearly, recording our experiences, and perhaps most importantly, by publicising our errors.

5. To contribute to the understanding of the problems of curriculum innovation generally.

Sources: Butcher and Pont[8]

As we stressed, this is a basic framework: much activity of an incidental and possible *ad hoc* nature will take place in and around it. This may comprise discussions among teachers, researchers and pupils; regular meetings among teachers or schools to discuss progress and problems, and to exchange information; possibly regional conferences; and related activities, all enhanced by the range of current hardware — tapes, video-recordings and transcripts.

❑ Conclusion: examples of action research in the field of curriculum development

So far in our review of action research as a method, we have touched upon its principal characteristics, occasions when it may be used, conceptual issues and the stages of its implementation. Another important feature which we have only mentioned in passing concerns the problems and difficulties encountered in mounting this kind of project, especially when on a fairly ambitious scale. It is these problems and difficulties which help to give this particular methodology its special flavour. Often unforeseen, and therefore not prepared for, they are as valuable for what can be learned from them as are the planned aspects of a project. We conclude this chapter, then, with a problem-oriented look at two action research-based project of some magnitude which have been undertaken in the field of curriculum research and development in recent years — the Humanities Curriculum Project and the Keele Integrated Studies Project.

The first of these, the Humanities Curriculum Project, was set up in 1967 under the joint sponsorship of the Schools Council and the Nuffield Foundation. Its aim and premises we have listed in Figure 5.1. The overall task of the project was to discover a teaching strategy which would implement these premises in the classroom, to report this strategy, and to support teachers who wished to develop it with training and if necessary with materials.

The problems and difficulties in mounting this project appear to have stemmed in the main from mistaken or incongruent attitudes and expectations on the part of the teachers in the experimental schools. Thus, their initial outlook tended to be coloured by earlier, more traditional approaches to the curriculum based on single-subject specialisms with the emphasis on improving teaching methods in these fields. They failed to appreciate that the venture had a social science basis and that they would need to adopt a suitably detached stance in keeping with its experimental nature. Having this kind of basis, the project was seen by the researchers as a means of testing hypotheses; many of the teachers, however, in awe of the presumed authority of the Schools Council, its sponsors, felt that they themselves were on trial. As a result, some of the experimental feedback was distorted. Misunderstandings with respect to the researchers' time perspective was another source of difficulty. The research team was concerned with long-term development; yet they were often perceived as attempting an instant and easy solution to problems. Finally, the teachers in the experimental schools tended to harbour feelings that the project would in some way help to solve problems of discipline and control. As it was, 'It made them more acute [and] opened them up instead of containing them'.[8]

The second example of the use of action research is that of the Keele Integrated Studies Project initiated in 1969. Notwithstanding the success of the project and the value of the accrued experience in implementing it, we here again restrict ourselves to some of the more problematic aspects. Difficulties arose once more from the way the project was perceived or misperceived by the teachers in the experimental schools, as well as from the ambiguous relationship they had with it (we refer you to Figure 5.3 which lists the metaphors selected by one of the parties involved to describe the teachers' perceptions of the project). We will, however, focus our remarks on the problem of communication between teachers and researchers which seemed to persist throughout the undertaking.

Efforts on the part of the research team to inform the schools at the outset of the project's objectives by means of meetings, conferences and circulars met with sustained complaints from the teachers about jargon and the lack of specific advice. The latter at this stage were indifferent to the researchers' attempts to explain the principles of integration and theories of curriculum development. This bears out the point we made earlier about rival characterisations of teaching and research. Subsequently, however, after having experienced the practical difficulties of implementing integrated studies, the teachers reversed their complaint, demanding explanation and theoretical reasoning for what they were doing. The discrepancy between what they requested and what they were prepared to do resulted in a lasting tension. As Shipman[9] points out, they wanted 'both academic rigour and easy-bake recipes from the same source'.

A further serious problem, yet another aspect of the communication gap, arose from the low priority given by the teachers to feedback. To this may be added their general reluctance to seek advice. In spite of the provision made by the researchers, only two out of the thirty-eight schools involved provided regular feedback to the research team. As Shipman again observes, this omission may be traced to the fact that the definitions of the project team and of the teachers were at different levels; 'The teachers were involved with their own problems and defined the project out of their own experience in their own classrooms. As a consequence the basic principles behind the project were usually misunderstood and often unconsidered'.

We see from this that what is involved is group process and that this is not easy to handle. Favourable conditions for action research include the following: a willingness on the part of the teachers to admit limitations and to make themselves familiar with the basic techniques of research; the provision of opportunities to invent; the encouragement of new ideas; the provision of time for experimentation; a mutual trust of those involved; and a knowledge on the part of the participants of the fundamentals of group processes. Additionally, it must be realised that many minds working on the same problem will increase the number of ways of looking at it. There will be more suggested solutions and more effective criticisms of each proposed solution. It must also be recognised that action research involved a re-education of teachers; that their attitudes and values will need to change; that the longer they have been in the job, the more difficult for secondary teachers (as opposed to primary teachers) because they are less used to working together.

In conclusion it might be added that in a representative sample of action research studies conducted in the United States, it was found[5] that the teachers taking part were generally enthusiastic. They seemed to feel that the staff worked more as a unit than before the research, the staff members were drawn closer together with the knowledge that they shared problems and goals, and that respect for individuals, both teachers and pupils, had increased.

❏ References

1. Halsey, A.H. (Ed) (1972) *Educational Priority: EPA Problems and Policies*, 1, London: HMSO

2. *Association for Supervision and Curriculum Development. Learning about Learning from Action Research* (1959) Washington DC: National Educational Association of the United States

3. Corey, S.M. (1953) *Action Research to Improve School Practices*, New York: Bureau of Publications, Teachers College, Columbia University

4. See, for example: Brown, R.K. (1967) 'Research and consultancy in industrial enterprises: a review of the contribution of the Tavistock Institute of Human Relations to the development of Industrial Sociology'. *Sociology*, 1, 1 33–60

5. Hodgkinson, H.L. (1957) 'Action Research — a critique'. *J. Educ. Sociol*, 31, 4 137–53

6. Butcher, H.J. and Pont, H.B. (1973) (Eds) *Educational Research in Britain 3*, London: University of London Press

7. Hill, J.E. and Kerber, A. (1967), *Methods and Analytical Procedures in Educational Research*, Detroit: Wayne State University Press

8. Stenhouse, L. 'The humanities curriculum project' in Butcher and Pont, op. cit. *Educational Research in Britain 3*

9. Shipman, D.D. (1974) *Inside a Curriculum Project*, London: Methuen

10. Travers, R.M.W., Extract quoted in Halsy op. cit. (Ed), *Educational Priority*

11. Marris, P. and Rein, M. (1967) *Dilemmas of Social Reform: Poverty and Community Action in the United States*, London: Routledge and Kegan Paul

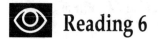 **Reading 6**

Formulating Questions for Questionnaires

Kane, E. (1985) *Doing your own Research,* London: Marion Boyars

[...] **Problem questions:** there are a number of traps to avoid when you write your questions. Some of them are based on common sense, but others might strike you only when you get baffling or useless replies on your questionnaire. For example:

- **the Double Question:** 'Do you walk to school or carry your lunch?' the wording of some questions make them difficult or impossible to answer accurately. Sometimes they contain two or more unrelated or even contradictory parts, the answers to which may be different: 'Are you happy in your marriage and job?' some are simply confusing: 'Would you agree that it is not unlikely that our next mayor won't be a woman?' A question that to you seems extra-carefully worded may be a mind-bender to your respondents.

- **the Wrong-Choice Question:** 'Is your hair yellow, purple, green or blue?' Pre-testing your questions on a practice group will help to ensure that you give your respondents appropriate questions and all the relevant choices of answers. Horse sense often is not enough here, for what may appear bizarre or unthinkable behaviour to you (and therefore ignored in your questionnaire) may be a way of life to some of your respondents.

- **the Kitchen Sink Question:** 'Please list all the places you have worked in the past five years, the type of work done and salary received, and why you left.' To save confusion in replying, recording and coding the answers ask each part of the question separately.

- **the 'Fuzzy Word' Question:** 'Should middle-aged people live it up?' there are two problems here. 'Middle-aged' does not mean the same age group to everyone, and 'living it up' can mean anything from wearing red to keeping a harem. Fuzzy words can creep into almost any question: 'Do you attend dances frequently?' (or 'rarely' or 'occasionally' or 'often') will give meaningless answers.

- **the Cover-the-World Question:** 'What do you think of the President?' could refer to the man personally, his job performance, or his status as president of the nation. 'What's this neighbourhood like?' is useful in some interviews (see emic interviews) but if you know what aspect of the neighbourhood interests you, ask specifically about that.

- **Jargon Questions:** 'Do you feel that your husband has a self-actualising autonomous personality structure?' is an affront to the respondent as well as to the English language. Also, be careful about words which have one meaning to the professionals in your field and another, or none, to the public. 'Culture', 'personality', 'role', or 'institution' cannot be treated as if all respondents share a common understanding of the professional meaning you intended.

  More generally, the language and style of the questionnaire must be comfortable to the respondent. 'Writing down' is insulting, and using dialect or 'in' words to reach a group of which you are obviously not a member is usually inappropriate.

- **'Dream' Questions:** hypothetical questions do not necessarily produce comparable answers from different respondents. 'What kind of education would you like for your child?' might produce a 'sky's the limit' answer from a person who is stating his absolute ideal; from another person, you might receive a modest statement of the best he or she thinks the child is likely to get. Make sure you know whether your question examines wishes or expectations.

- **Leading Questions:** 'Why are you happy here in Newtown?' or 'Why do you think the community looks up to doctors?' gives the respondent little opening to say he is miserable in Newtown and thinks that most of the people in his community feel that doctors are charlatans.

- **'Heresay' Questions:** 'Do you think your neighbours are happy about the new school?' Do not ask one person the opinions or attitudes of another, unless you wish to compare the first person's impressions with facts which you will establish from the second person. You cannot cut down on your population numbers by asking a small number of people what they think the attitudes of other people might be.

- **'Fall-out' Questions:** these are sets of questions in which something important gets lost on the way. Here is real-life example: a woman who normally dyes her hair red went to a hairdresser who required that his clients fill out a questionnaire before getting their hair done. Bad dyes of any colour will turn hair red. The questionnaire asked:

1. Do you colour your hair?   Yes.......... No..........
2. If yes, does it ever turn red   Yes.......... No..........
3. If yes, what product do you use? ....

The conclusion which the hairdresser drew was that anyone who answered 'yes' to Question 2 was using bad hair dye — a conclusion which was invalidated by all the women who purposely dyed their hair red.

Finally it is obvious that if uninfluenced answers are required, you do not put questions in the form of 'You don't think ..., do you? (Moser and Kalton 1971, 308). But the researcher's biases and preferences can be projected in more subtle ways. In our example of neighbourhood mothers with children under five years of age, the focus of inquiry might be their views about adult educational opportunities for themselves, and their aspirations for their children. The wording of these questions can easily imply that adult education or certain kinds of educational aspirations are something the *researcher* values, and therefore the mother may feel she is expected to make particular choices. [...]

❏ Reference

Moser, C.A. and Kalton, G (1971) *Survey Methods in Social Investigation*, 2nd Edn. Aldershot: Gower

 **Reading 7**

Bias in Surveys Caused by Non-response

Hoinville, R., Jowell, R. et al. (1978) *Survey Research Practice*, London: Heinemann

[...]

❑ Coping with non-response

Despite all the efforts at maximizing response levels, some recipients will not reply. In fact, non-response in postal surveys takes two forms: failure to return the questionnaire, and failure to answer one or more of the questions. The latter is usually referred to as item non-response. The reasons for it will seldom be clear but if the questionnaire has been well-designed and pretested it is unlikely to occur frequently. We concentrate here on the more common and more important problem of failure to respond at all.

Non-response is peculiarly important in postal surveys because there are generally no clues about the characteristics of non-respondents and how they differ from respondents. In field surveys, interviewers can often collect limited information about non-respondents such as approximate age, house type, type of area. Moreover, the evidence available suggests that respondents and non-respondents to postal surveys do differ in several respects.

Respondents (and particularly early respondents) tend to be:

- favourably disposed towards the survey's aims or involved in the survey subject
- politically or socially active
- in the higher socio-economic groups
- receptive to new ideas
- rapid decision-makers
- high achievers, especially educationally
- used to communicating by post.

Non-respondents and late respondents are more likely to:

- be elderly, disengaged or withdrawn
- live in urban, rather than suburban or rural areas

- feel that they may be judged by the responses that they make
- feel that they will be inadequate at supplying the information requested.

[...]

It is to mitigate some of these potential biasing factors that the initial contact with recipients is so important. But no matter how much effort is made to encourage response, the likelihood of more resistance (in postal and indeed in interview surveys) from most of the types of people listed above is very great indeed. And if the subject matter is related in any way to the characteristics associated with non-response the results will contain some element of bias.

Two kinds of checks on non-response can be carried out on most postal surveys. First, an analysis can be made of answers to key questions by date of reply (which should be coded onto the questionnaire). Early returns often yield a higher proportion of positive answers to one or more of the key questions than do later replies. By plotting the proportion of positive answers over time, an estimate can be made, by extrapolation, of the likely responses of those who did not respond at all. Second, the profile of respondents can be checked against known characteristics of the population sample, for instance, checks can be made against the census distributions of age and urban/rural populations.

A third check is available in rare cases when further information about the sample can be gained from independent records (chiefly the sampling frame) which may provide a more definitive picture of the characteristics of non-respondents.

When the characteristics of non-respondents can be established, consideration could be given to weighting the final sample by an appropriate factor in an attempt to reduce the bias. If it seems necessary and resources permit, a further reminder letter could be used to secure further returns. Where non-response is suspected of having a particularly damaging effect on the validity of the findings of a postal survey, the designer may need to conduct follow-up interviews with all or with a subsample of non-respondents, using a full or a shortened version of the questionnaire. [...]

 **Reading 8**

Semi-Structured Interviews

Johnson, D., and Ransom, E. (1983) *Family and School*, London: Croom Helm

❑ Appendix

❑ The substance of the interview

Our general aim was to elicit parents' perceptions about the role of a parent in the school life of the child, with a particular focus on the secondary school phase. However, in order to see if there was continuity in parental approach in the different stages of school life, we hoped also to enquire into what had been parents' responses to the primary school life of their child.

So far as possible we aimed to keep a balance between getting descriptive accounts from parents about their interaction with the school and obtaining their opinions about the appropriate role of the parent.

In order to achieve some systematic and comparable coverage of parent outlook in each interview, we formulated seven areas of enquiry which we would aim to cover. These were:

- primary school life
- choice of secondary school
- preliminary contact with secondary school
- expectations of the school
- interaction with the school
- the parent and the child
- the parent and outside agencies[1]

Often there was a topical and appropriate point of departure for the interview, for example, the recent choice of secondary school in the case of a first year child, the imminent school examination of an older pupil, or perhaps some recent encounter with a teacher. In the absence of any positive lead from the parents we would tend to begin with a look back at the primary school years, working on to the present day. We did not use tape recorders and indeed these would have been unsuitable in the far from quiet circumstances in which we often conducted our interviews. Background noises from aircraft, television and other family members would have been too intrusive for effective tape recording. Instead we took notes, using key words or phrases on our clipboards to remind us of areas of enquiry. Questions themselves were always spontaneously formulated to follow the flow of conversation and the parent's and interviewer's styles of speech.[2]

In a few cases a particularly urgent or topical issue would dominate discussion, for example a parent's dispute with a teacher, or the recent realignment of the parent/child relationship on a one-parent family basis. Very occasionally, family life was just too pressing for the full and leisurely exploration of past events. One interview took place within the compass of the preparation and cooking of a pan of chips. But these were the exceptions. Most of the interviews were sufficiently open-ended to enable coverage of all our areas of interest.

[...]

❏ Notes

1. By this we meant the various agencies being investigated in other sectors of our research, e.g. education welfare service, child guidance clinics etc.

2. While the interviewer made no attempt to imitate or adopt the vocabulary of the parent, care was taken not to introduce educational jargon or unfamiliar terms. One or two unexpected difficulties of communication presented themselves however, as for example the use of the generic term 'secondary' school. One mother felt herself to be ineligible for interview because ' they all go to these *comprehensives*' now.

 **Reading 9**

Probing in Semi-Structured Interviews

Hoinville, R. and Jowell, R. (1978) *Survey Research Practice*, London: Heinemann. pp. 101–102

[...]

❑ Probing

A key interviewing skill is probing: encouraging the respondent to give an answer or to clarify or amplify an answer. Probing may be non-verbal or verbal. An expectant glance at the respondent or a muttered 'mm' is a probe; so is a direct request such as 'Please tell me more about that', or 'What other reasons?' Probing should always be neutral, as opposed to prompting, which involves suggesting an answer to a respondent. Many questions are designed with specific prompts; this is a matter for the questionnaire designer, and interviewers ought never to prompt on their own initiative.

Several types of probes can be useful for precoded questions. Suppose the interviewer asks, for example, 'How satisfied are you with your present home? Would you say you are very satisfied, fairly satisfied, not very satisfied or not at all satisfied?' the answer may be 'I couldn't really say.' This answer does not usually mean that the respondent has no views but that he is hesitating between the categories offered. In such cases, the interviewer can probe with some such phrase as 'Which comes closest to your view?' and report the question. If the answer still does not fit a precoded (e.g. 'I suppose it's all right') the interviewer will need to repeat the relevant precodes ('Would you say you are very satisfied, fairly satisfied ...?' etc).

Probing is particularly important with open-ended questions, when the respondent is asked to express his views in his own words, and the interviewer has to record them in full. To get the respondent to expand his answer, the interviewer may use whichever of the following probes seems most appropriate; for some questions several may be needed:

- an expected glance
- 'uh-huh', 'mm' or 'yes' followed by an expectant silence
- 'What else?'
- 'Please tell me more about that.'
- 'I'm interested in all your reasons.'

Respondents often use ambiguous words such as 'important' in their answers, or make vague references: 'It is because of my health/my age/the state of the country.' The interviewer needs to seek clarification with probes such as:

- 'Exactly why do you think this is important?'
- 'How do you mean it's because of your age?'
- 'I don't quite understand what you mean by *important*.'
- 'In what ways does it affect your health?'

Whatever probes are used, the interviewer's task is clear: to draw out all relevant responses from respondents; to ensure that inarticulate or shy respondents have as much chance to give their opinions as articulate or talkative ones; to be neutral, interested and persuasive. Probing is an aspect of interviewing that requires great skill. If carried out poorly it can lead either to loss of information or to the collection of biased information. The skills of probing therefore feature prominently in interviewer training, but it requires experience in the field to refine and develop them.

 **Reading 10**

Guidelines for Interviews

Powney, J. and Watts, M. (1987) *Interviewing in Educational Research*, London: Routledge and Kegan Paul. pp. 176–177

[...]

❏ Checklist for reporting interviews in educational research

1. Kind and context of interview

   - What is the rationale for using interviews?
   - What kind of interview is it?
   - How is the interview structured?
   - How much flexibility does the interviewer have?
   - What is the length, location and occasion of the interview?

2. Characteristics of the interview participants

(a) Interviewees

   - Who and how many people are involved?
   - What is the basis for their selection and how was the selection made?

(b) Interviewers

   - Who and how many people are involved?
   - What experience of interviewing do they have?
   - What is their relationship to the main research?
   - What is their status and relationship to the interviewees?

3. The purpose of the interview

   - What are interviewees told about the purpose of the interview?
   - Is this understanding shared with the interviewer?
   - Who will have access to the data collected and is it negotiable?

4. The method(s) of data collection

    - How strictly controlled is the method of asking questions?
    - How are responses recorded?
    - What other methods of data collection are being used?
    - What is the relative weighting between the methods?

5. Analysis and reporting of data

    - Who analyses what?
    - How are the interviewers concerned with the analysis?
    - How many analysts are there and how are disagreements resolved?
    - Are full transcripts used?
    - What basis is used for filtering the data?
    - What level of uncodable or unsortable data is tolerated?

6. Sorting of results

    - How are the outcomes of the interviews being evaluated?
    - What access may the academic community have to raw data?

[...]

 **Reading 11**

Observation

Three articles from the *Cambridge Journal of Education*, (1987) **17**, 2, pp. 83–90

❏ The primary school staff relationships project: origins, aims and methods

Jennifer Nias, *Tutor in Curriculum Studies 3–13, Cambridge Institute of Education, and Director of the Primary School Staff Relationships Project*

Although the proposal for this project was written two and a half years ago, the ideas behind it had been growing steadily in my mind for three years before that. Work with teachers on a variety of courses at the Cambridge Institute of Education from 1977 onwards had convinced me of five related facts. First, teachers at all levels, including heads, were more deeply affected, for good or ill, by the adult relationships (including those with ancillary staff) in their schools than had generally been given public recognition, especially in the published literature on schools.

Secondly, they were often ill-equipped by temperament or training, to recognise or deal constructively with differences of opinion, value and practice between themselves or their colleagues or among the latter.

Thirdly, most of the management courses with which I was at that time familiar failed to address either of these two sets of circumstances as if they were problems which affected anyone in a school except perhaps its head. Staff relationships, if they figured at all on many of such courses, were not treated as if the staff themselves had a responsibility for them.

Fourthly, there was almost no published or unpublished literature on staff (teaching or ancillary) relationships. What there was was written about or from the perspective of the headteacher, or was drawn from studies of secondary schools, and none of it portrayed the adults in schools as individuals, facing day-to-day interactions under circumstances which critically affected their motivation, job-satisfaction and effectiveness in the classroom.

Lastly, the majority of English primary schools have 5–10 teaching staff, a number which is that of a classic small group (Agazarian and Peters, 1981). Yet there was no information available as to whether or not such staff behaved as groups and, if they did, to what extent and in what ways it affected them.

Then several developments occurred almost simultaneously. The management of primary schools became a high profile activity; in a national situation of dwindling resources for education some money was available for INSET for primary heads. With encouragement from its Director, Howard Bradly, the Institute expanded its hitherto scanty provision in this area and in 1983 a new post was created for a tutor in Primary Education and Management. Geoff Southworth joined the staff from a primary headship and the primary management wagon began to roll in earnest. In the meantime, with help from Jane Abercrombie and Bill Lintott from Cambridge Group Work, I had begun to run courses for teachers (at all levels and from all types of school) on topics such as staff relationships, leadership and communication in the staff group and collaborative work among teachers. Furthermore, as the debate about specialisation in primary schools became more heated, recognition was growing throughout the education system that inter-adult relationships affected the way in which many teachers, not just curriculum coordinators, carried out their responsibilities.

It is no coincidence then that the project itself should have been conceived in the Institute car park one morning in 1984, during the course of a brief conversation between Geoff Southworth and myself. Even then the idea might never have gone any further had the Economic and Social Research Council not advertised in the autumn calling, as part of their national initiative on teacher education, for bids for research proposals. Galvanised by a deadline into frenetic activity we wrote our proposal, greatly encouraged by the fact that Robin Yeomans, a local headteacher who had just joined the Institute as a Research Associate undertaking his own enquiry into primary school staff as groups, was available and willing to join us as a full-time Research Fellow.

Given the dearth of public knowledge on staff relationships of any kind and the fact that we wanted people to be able to make constructive use on initial and in-service courses of the information we gained from the research, we decided to focus on six schools in which teachers were working well together. We agreed that schools which 'offered a positive model of adult relationships' would enable us to learn what, for example, teachers, headteachers and ancillary staff actually do when they work constructively together, what attitudes they hold to each other and to their work, what kinds of leadership are associated with productive teamwork. We were also constrained by ethical considerations: we wanted eventually to make our work public and we had therefore to gain the permission of all the staff in each school that we studied to the inclusion of our observations and interviews in any future reports and case studies. Common sense dictated that such a sensitive enterprise would be best undertaken in schools which enjoyed relationships characterised by openness and trust and not by conflict and disharmony.

It could reasonably be argued that research into schools where 'good staff relationships' already existed would be limited in scope and usefulness. Leaving aside the fact that in a state of almost total public ignorance, one has to start somewhere, one can however also focus on the potential usefulness to the profession of examples of 'good practice' (a fact strongly endorsed in 1986 by the Select Committee Report on 'Achievement in Primary Schools'). It may in the long run be of greater help to teachers who know what characterises primary schools as organizations when its members work well together than to publish accounts (such as that by Hartley, 1986) of staff groups paralysed by tacit dissension.

Geoff Southworth's article describes in further detail the process by which the six schools were selected. Although we were not looking for schools which were representative in any statistical sense, we hoped to find ones which differed in a number of respects (e.g. experienced and inexperienced heads, open-plan and cellular buildings, staffs with varying proportions of more or less experienced members, single- and mixed-sex staffs, different types of catchment area, voluntary and maintained schools) which our experience suggested might be significant. In the event, the schools we studied exhibited most of these differences and were from three local authorities. Overall, they had little in common in terms of structure, organization and pupil intake, apart from their size (from 6–10 teaching staff, a caretaker, a secretary and at least one ancillary worker).

We had no doubts what the general nature of our methodology should be. First, it had to be qualitative and ethnographic rather than quantitative, since there was no way in which so-called objective measures could capture the lived realities of adults' lives in schools. Secondly, we took the view of Hammersley and Atkinson (1983) that 'any account of human behaviour requires that we understand the social meanings that inform it'. We had therefore to become, as nearly as we could, members of staff ourselves, hoping that as participant observers we could come to understand the culture and communication of the groups we were joining and believing that as outsiders we certainly could not. Thirdly, we felt we needed to work (as part-time teachers) in the schools for a full academic year, in order to allow time for the staff and children to accept us and so that we could include evidence from periods characterised by different types of activity and levels of intensity (e.g. Christmas, the end of the summer term, periods of staff illness, staff changes).

It was also clear that the first outcome of our fieldwork should be case studies, for these would be the most likely form of product to capture with veri-similitude the rich, varied, dense and crowded lives and interactions of the staff members. In deciding how to tackle the case studies we were guided by the work of Eliott (1981) and Stenhouse (1982), though we decided not to create separate case records ('an ordered selection from the data', Stenhouse, 1978, p. 33) believing that the data included in the studies would be full enough to speak for themselves. We felt that the shape and nature of each case study should be determined by its writer in response to the unique features of that school, provided that its structure was grounded in the evidence and that there was detailed description aimed to produce case studies which were analytic but rich in first-hand accounts.

The process by which the main themes in each school's case study emerged is documented by the reflective comments each of us included in his/her fieldnotes and by the transcripts of our recorded monthly, three-hour team meetings. We did not intend that the case studies should include accounts of the development of our thinking about the schools, since each study was designed in the first instance to offer a mirror of its own practices to a specific school. We did not wish to distort this image with our own methodological considerations. As a result, the case studies present an illusory picture of tidy thinking and precise analysis. In fact, as we worked out our plans for each case study, individually and together, we were muddled, frustrated, tortuous and repetitive, discarding as much material and almost as many ideas as we finally included.

But this is to anticipate. Before the case studies could be compiled, we had to find possible schools, gain access to them, conduct fieldwork in them for the full length of a school year and negotiate clearance of our material. Geoff Southworth's article in this issue describes the first two of these processes, Robin Yeomans' the last. The main forms of evidence which we used in our fieldwork were documentary analyses (e.g. of school brochures, curriculum statements, governors' reports), fieldnotes and interviews. Fieldnotes were taken on the spot, unobtrusively or out of sight, in small notebooks which we always carried with us. A full version was then dictated at the end of the day and subsequently transcribed by one of the many patient secretaries to whose skill and perseverance we are greatly indebted. Note-taking and making continued throughout the year, though we all found that our fieldnotes changed in nature as we began to 'progressive(ly) focus' (Glaser and Strauss, 1967). At first, we recorded copiously, taking note of anything which might be relevant. Over time, we tended to be more selective, to collect information on limited topics and to take for granted some of the aspects of school life which had initially struck us. For this reason, it was useful from time to time to re-read one's earlier fieldnotes, to regain the sense of strangeness which had once characterised the now-familiar.

Indeed, we found it hard to avoid the well-known hazard facing all participant observers, that of 'going native'. As we became members of staff it was increasingly difficult not to identify completely with the school's life and interests. The cutting edge of observation and analysis can easily be blunted by over-involvement in individuals' daily crises, or in particular curicula or pedagogical problems. We had constantly to struggle against the temptation to become so fully insiders that we lost the outsider's ability to record and comment with detachment.

For the most part, interviews were conducted towards the end of the school year, though they were also used earlier on to document particular events or milestones (e.g. when staff left or joined a school or the deputy took the head's place while the latter was ill). Almost all the interviews took place in school, many during school time. All but two were tape-recorded, with the interviewees' permission, and transcripts were subsequently handed back to them for checking and clearance. Interviews were loosely structured round key questions which were specific to the circumstance of each school but interviewees were encouraged to talk as freely and for as long as they wished. They also had the right to turn off the tape-recorder, if they so desired. Interviews varied in length from forty minutes to two hours.

In each school we noted that our relationship with the staff changed once we had started to interview in earnest. Although it took varying lengths of time for us to be absorbed into different schools, and although it would be naive to claim that our presence did not affect staff interactions and relationships, we both felt that the staff in all the schools allowed us to be as unobtrusive as we individually wished and that we were accepted by them. For much of the academic year, for much of the time, the ancillary and teaching staff of an individual school appeared to forget that we were researchers — until the tape-recorders appeared.

Indispensable as the interviews were in offering fresh perspectives and new information, they were also therefore more self-conscious and possibly therefore more constrained than informal conversations held in the corridor, the staffroom or the teaching area.

As I write this, we are about to start generating from the six case studies issues which are common to them all. These, illustrated by material from the case studies, will form the basis of a book, *Understanding the Primary School as an Organization* (provisional title), to be published by Holt Rinehart (Cassell) as soon as we can find time to write it. We feel we have something new to say which will be of use to teachers, headteachers, teacher educators and administrators. We hope readers of this Journal will feel that too.

❏ References

Agarzarian, Y. and Peters, R. (1981) *The Visible and Invisible Groups*, London: Routledge and Kegan Paul.

Elliott, J. (1981) 'The Cambridge accountability project'. *Cambridge Journal of Education*, **11**, 2, 146–166.

Glaser, B and Strauss, A. (1967) *The Discovery of Grounded Theory*, London: Weidenfield and Nicholson.

Hammersley, M and Atkinson, P. (1983) *Ethnography: Principles in Practice*, London: Tavistock Press.

Hartly, D. (1986) *Understand the Primary School*, London: Croom Helm.

Stenhouse, L. (1978) 'Case study and case records: towards a contemporary history of education'. *British Educational Research Journal*, **4**, 2, 21–39.

Stenhouse, L. (1982) 'The conduct, analysis and report of case study in educational research and evaluation' in McCormick, R. et al. (Eds) *Calling Education to Account*, London: Heinemann.

❏ The experience of fieldwork: or insider dealings, who profits?

Geoff Southworth, *Tutor in Primary Education and Management, Cambridge Institute of Education, and Primary School Staff Relationships Project Team Member*

Later in April 1985 we heard that the Economic and Social Research Council (ESRC) had awarded us a grant to carry out research into Primary School Staff Relationships (PSSR). We were, of course, delighted to 'get the money' but by the time the letter confirming the grant arrived we had less than ten weeks in which to contact LEAS, approach schools, explain the project and find six schools to work in.

Research staff relationships sounds rather more straightforward than it is. Jennifer Nias' and Robin Yeomans' companion articles to this should provide details of the aims of the project and methodological issues. Nevertheless, it will be useful to quote some of our publicity to provide a flavour as to what we were attempting:

> The Project will seek to understand the medium-sized primary school (head and teaching staff of six to twelve and at least three non-teaching staff) as an adult organization and to identify the structures, behaviours and culture which characterise schools in which head, teaching and ancillary staff work productively together.

> The research will take the form of case studies of the teaching and ancillary staff in six primary schools which offer a positive model of adult relationships. The Project team will work throughout the academic year as part-time teachers in the schools and, as participant-observers, will use qualitative research methods. The case studies will be validated by the participants and, where appropriate, will be modified in response to their comments. The schools have been selected to give as wide as possible a variety of organisational forms, buildings, catchment areas, types and length of staff experience, but are not intended to be representative.

Of the many things which could be focused on from this extract I will attempt to describe some aspects of being a participant observer.

The notion of participant observation is inherently schizophrenic. At any one time we were simultaneously part-time teachers in the school (participants) and investigators and recorders of what we witnessed, heard, and experienced (observers). Although the duality of the role was sometimes difficult I think all three of us would now acknowledge that the project has benefited considerably from our adoption of this role. I say this because our felt perceptions, the emotional content of living inside a school, the shared experiences with teacher ancillary colleagues in 'our' respective schools and the first-hand experience of teaching in the schools enriched and informed our thinking about the schools as organisations and the relationships which create and sustain those six schools. However, all of these claims rest upon the assumption that we did live *inside* each of the six schools. How did we gain access to those schools? And how did we get inside them?

During the summer term of 1985 seven LEAs within a 100 mile round trip of Cambridge agreed to us approaching some of their schools. By an extensive process of visiting and explaining we found a group of schools interested in the project, and willing to have one of us join the staff. It should be noted at this point that the initial selection process had to be mutual — not only should we want to work in the school but that school had to want us to work with them. Moreover, by 'school' we meant *all* the staff group — teachers, caretaker, ancillaries, secretary. Therefore gaining access meant a series of discussions with heads, staff groups and individuals. By July we had found and gained access to six schools so that we were ready to enter the schools in September. However, it is probably true to say that our experience of approaching those schools involved an initial period of selection which was both more protracted and thorough than the usual staff selection process of application, visit and interview. Consequently, we arrived in post having already begun the process of joining the staff. For us selection was not simply appointment, it also included induction since our entry was mutually negotiated with all members of the school.

Joining the school in September therefore was something of a second phase activity, but nevertheless it is a topic worthy of investigation. The experience certainly provided some valuable data. In my case I was warmly welcomed; even before I had got out of the car the head was shaking my hand and welcoming me to the school. I was offered coffee and all staff were smiling and helping to put me at my ease. I must confess the exuberance made me think that I was being treated as a special case: the researcher-as-mascot of the school's worth? Yet over the first few weeks this suspicion was refuted — everyone in that school is welcomed. Watching how other visitors were received became one element in the collection of data and I found all were treated consistently in the same way. What was extended to me was part of the school's code of consideration and courtesy.

Joining the school is not, though, the same as 'getting into' the school. I had crossed the threshold and passed some courtesy tests but 'getting-in' involves surviving the 'rites de passage' of credibility. All three of us engaged on the project feel we were put through some sort of 'test'. The most obvious are those of proving one's worth as a teacher. A teacher's classroom performance matters, certainly in 'our' six schools, and I suspect in many others. Other researchers have remarked on similar such tests (Popplewell, 1986) and/or have agreed with this notion of induction as, in part, involving a series of credibility tests (Southworth, 1987). One of the benefits we brought to the school was that of being an 'extra teacher', since we were supernumerary to the LEA's pupil-teacher ratio. Consequently the schools could employ us as they thought appropriate. We were, in effect, supply teachers in regular attendance. Therefore, I was often engaged on a rotating basis. This week four- and five-year-olds, next week ten-year-olds, the week after seven- and eight-year-olds. I certainly got around the school and had to demonstrate competence with the full primary age range. It was not always comfortable, particularly at first, when I was working in unfamiliar classrooms, with classes of children whose names I did not know. One by-product of this research is that I now know I would not like to be a supply teacher.

Such challenges and discomforts apart, though, the experience provided some important insights. For example, I soon knew what it was like to teach in each and every classroom. This gave insights into the nature of the building, and the effect that physical layout of the school might have on each individual teacher and member of staff. I also became aware of inter-classroom communications, which rooms were most visited and by whom. I was soon able to talk to each teacher, and frequently the ancillary and support staff, about the key issues of the job — the class of children, materials, equipment, lesson plans and projects, and individual children (illnesses, progress, special needs, interests, the things children said, children's work etc). Within a few days of going to the school I was able to join in and speak the school's language. Learning the language is very important when you visit other lands and other schools.

'Getting in', though, was not solely dependent upon teaching competence and the learning of the school's patois. There were the social mores and personal values to observe. I have already mentioned the quality of welcome and that serves as one example. I found myself welcoming other visitors as I was welcomed. Other mores would be coffee in the staffroom particularly before and after school, a sense of humour, being willing and able to laugh at oneself, displaying concerns for colleagues both as professionals and as persons, and offering and accepting advice. Such things might seem to be only an informal series of tests but they are actually the ways in which any individual member fits in with the staff group, as I discovered when I enquired into teacher selection (Southworth, 1987). Moreover they are some of the ways in which an individual becomes a *member* of a team and how a team develops into a group (Yeomans, 1986 and 1987).

Most of these ideas are derived from post-event analysis of what we saw and heard in the school. In one sense they are presented in too straightforward a way and may imply that these things are easily observed and simple to discover. I believe that they appear to be 'straightforward' now because I have a clarity of vision that only comes with hindsight, and from sharing and refining the data with my project colleagues. At the time my vision was much more impaired and partial. Nor would I claim that my perceptions now are not partial or impaired; they are! I would only claim to have a less imperfect view now, but certainly not 20/20 vision.

Collecting data was not easy. I had to learn to listen and to look. I have mentioned the learning of a language and in some ways that is an appropriate metaphor. However, the language I learned was both oral and visual. There is a considerable amount of non-verbal communication in schools. Moreover it is usually fleeting and subtle. A grimace across the staffroom and intended only for one's friend could mean almost anything. Similarly raised eyebrows, nods, vacant stares, shrugs and many other signals have their own meanings dependent upon the individual displaying them. I learned to see these signals but cracking the code was much harder. For that reason the use of formal interviews was immensely valuable and helped me to make sense of the things I had observed but often could not understand.

Much the same applies to talk. For one thing I underestimated the problems of attempting to cope with concurrent talk. How do you deal with four or five conversations all taking place at the same time in the same staffroom? Furthermore, which conversations are the significant ones? Very quickly I gave up the pursuit of the significant and special and took all events and actions to be of significance. Obviously this meant I missed some things but it reduced my sense of being overwhelmed and overloaded. In fact many significant events 'found me'. Staff would report events that took place whilst I was away from the school: they would brief me, up-date me or explain why something was taking place. The staff were very considerate and tolerant of things I wanted to know.

Recording all this material was a rather different challenge. The greatest problem I encountered was that typically I was trying to note some conversation or event at the very time when I was supposed to be commencing a lesson. Thinking about teaching when trying to record research data was something of a headache. Often my lessons had delayed or stalled starts whilst I hurriedly scribbled a note to myself. The combination of participant and observer can mean that we are sometimes both a weaker participant and a constrained observer. Rather quickly I improved at recording. Often all I needed was to jot a line or two in my notebook. It was essential, though, at the end of each day in school to make detailed fieldnotes. Using my cryptic jottings as an *aide-mémoire* I would talk into the cassette-recorder, sometimes for long periods, recording what I had seen, and heard, and also what I felt and experienced.

A valuable part of fieldwork were the routine meetings with project colleagues. At least once a month the three of us met to compare notes. Usually these meetings lasted a full morning. A small amount of time was given over to administrative concerns but the bulk of the time was devoted to talking about our data. All of us had a lot of data to 'process'. Whilst the dictation of fieldnotes each evening after school tended to include some processing of the data, it was a solitary affair. In the team meetings we could compare the contrast notes and ideas, and come to some formative hypotheses. Perhaps more importantly, in the first term, we could learn from one another about looking and listening. It should also be mentioned that these regular team meetings provided support for the three of us. Although we all 'fitted into' our schools, and became members of the schools, it was encouraging to discover that colleague researchers were encountering similar issues and were struggling to cope with the same challenges. As participant observers 'adopted' by the host schools you are, by definition, not isolated or lonely at least whilst in the school. However, as researcher in the evening you are somewhat independent and it was helpful to have regular opportunities to share research concerns and hunches. Such discussions also meant we could progressively focus, but my point here is that as fieldworker you may need support. We each had a lot to talk about and it was important to be able to talk to someone.

We did, of course, also talk with the schools' staff. We conducted interviews with all staff, sometimes two or three interviews with certain staff. During those occasions we obviously shared our thoughts and observations and gathered in perspectives which gave new meanings or cast new lights and shadows on what we thought we were seeing. Moreover, we also handed back to all staff transcripts of their interviews so they could 'clear' the material and remove anything they felt uncomfortable with. Similarly, our case studies were cleared by all members of staff. I state this here because it might be construed from the above that we became research 'moles' rather than fieldworkers. If so, as Le Carré (1974) notes when his own mole-catcher, George Smiley, is first despatched, 'who spies on the spies'. Or in our case, who researches the researchers? The best people to do this are the staff we 'researched'. Hence the case studies were not only cleared by the staff but also checked by them, chiefly on the basis that '... one must be ready to handle the criticisms of those who actually live this life. The closer they think you come to describing it, the better you can feel about your data gathering, your organisation and your analysis' (Wiseman, 1979, quoted in Coulson, 1986).

Another metaphor to use for our fieldwork might be that of the Stock Exchange and insider dealings. Maybe we, as fieldworkers, were insider dealers: if so, who profits? Quite clearly we did, yet this note sent to me by a teacher on reading the case study of her school suggests that others also profit:

> I've just this minute finished your study. I think you've done a fine job on us — warts and all. I meant only to read for half- an- hour or so but I couldn't put it down.

> There were times when I wondered if there was 'anything in it for us' last year. I've learned a lot — both from the experience of the interviews and from reading the whole work.

❑ References

Le Carré, J. (1974) *Tinker, Tailor, Soldier, Spy*, London: Pan.

Popplewell, P. (1986) 'The experience of teaching in 'disadvantaged' areas in the UK and USA'. BERA conference paper, Bristol.

Southworth, G.W. (1987) 'Staff selection or by appointment? A case study of the appointment of a teacher to a primary school' in Southworth, G.W. (Ed) *Readings in Primary School Management*, Lewes: Falmer Press (forthcoming).

Wiseman, J.P. (1979) 'The research web' in Bynner, J. and Stribley, K.M. (Eds) *Social Research: Principles and Procedures*, Sheffield: Longman. pp. 113–21 cited in Coulson, A.A. (1986) *The Managerial Work of Primary School Headteachers*, Sheffield Papers in Education Management No. 48. Sheffield: Sheffield City Polytechnic.

Yeomans, R.Y. (1986) 'A different way of dancing? An alternative perspective on leading and belonging to a primary staff group'. *Cambridge Journal of Education*, **16**, 3, pp. 216–220

Yeomans, R.Y. (1987) 'Leading the team belonging to the group?' in Southworth, G.W. (Ed) *Readings in Primary School Management*, Lewes: Falmer Press (forthcoming).

❑ Checking and adjusting the lens: case study clearance

Robin Yeomans, *Primary School Staff Relationships Project Research Fellow*

As a full-time Research Fellow on the Primary School Staff Relationships Project I was a participant observer of the staff of four schools. Writing four case studies took me many long and lonely weeks. The experience was one of being successively preoccupied, worried, elated, tired in response to stimuli which had nothing to do with the world in which I was living and which had little meaning for others around me — except that it meant the decorating still didn't get done!

My point is that a case study writer can arrive at the clearance stage in a frame of mind which considers that the hard work has been completed. There is a danger that clearance can be seen as a phase which should be negotiated as rapidly as possible. There is the additional temptation to see oneself as owner of a document on which so much emotional energy has been expended. The case study writer becomes 'close' to the infant through gestation and uncomfortable birth. Hence it is difficult to achieve the psychological distance needed to judge how participants will react to seeing themselves through others' eyes. In the PSSR Project ownership rights are unequivocally shared with the participants in the individual schools. Thus clearing becomes a necessary lengthy process of negotiation to reconcile research and ethical considerations.

From a research stance clearance is a well established means of validating the perceptions collected in the case studies (Hammersley and Atkinson, 1983). By sharing our perceptions we could triangulate them with those of the staff we were researching. This did not mean that we were asking for blanket confirmation that we had correctly focused. Since the case studies made extensive use of field note and interview extracts, they sought to reflect the perceptions of the writer and of the participants. This clearing involves checking all these perceptions. In particular it was important to ensure that extracting portions from long interviews and inserting them in a case study context did not distort original meanings.

From an ethical stance we knew that relationships were a personally sensitive area of research that could and should only be explored with safeguards. The ethical code given to all participants confirmed that (amongst other safeguards) participants have a right to control the use to which accounts and recordings of situations are put; participants have a right to control the researcher's use of their interview material; the researcher has a responsibility to ensure that participants understand the context in which he/she proposes to use their interview data.

An additional safeguard was the anonymising of case studies so that the schools were not identifiable to external audiences. However, by the time staff were being interviewed it was evident that they were concerned equally about the impact of their contributions on their colleagues within the school.

There were potentially sensitive issues in some of the schools. The LEA's perception that each school offered 'a positive model of staff relationships' was not a guarantee of perfection nor an insurance policy against future changes. In particular, industrial action and staff changes were a feature of most of the schools. Clearance was intended to ensure that the school would be at least as healthy after reading the case study as before. The members of the team were agreed that ethical considerations had priority over research ones. There could be little gain in causing schools to feel they never again wanted to allow researchers across their thresholds.

In the time between completing field work and returning to clear case studies each school had altered. The staff group's membership had changed, sometimes extensively. We were already negotiating a historical document which could contain issues the staff had decided to bury. We were competing with the new preoccupations of a new school year for the limited time individuals had away from their classes. Sometimes it was possible to arrange the classes were covered whilst staff read and cleared interview extracts. Alternatively we had to compete with the other demands on staff at lunchtimes and after school. When staff had moved schools, there were visits to distant places; though in one instance the postal service was reluctantly preferred to a visit to the south coast.

There were three clearance phases. Firstly each participant was given a copy of their full interview transcripts to amend and release for use in the case study. With the case study first draft completed, times were arranged to show and explain to individuals their case study interview and field note extracts. The problem was to explain the context of extracts in the time available without compromising the confidentiality of other participants. One system was to colour code each individual's contributions, list the pages, and clear each entry page by page. Once all participants had been consulted individually and adjustments had been agreed, the full amended version of the case study was given to everyone in the school. They could then respond to and subsequently clear the full document individually or collectively, depending on the circumstances of each school and individual. This tidy sounding process could take several weeks and might be uncomfortable, illuminating, and productive at different times.

As researchers selecting from a vast quantity of interview and field note data we had tried to take account of participant reactions to exposure, though each case study was organised with research implications in mind. We were more perceptive in some instances than in others.

Many participants made no adjustments when clearing individually, though a few found intimidating the prospect of releasing transcript extracts from what had felt like informal conversations. Some found their speech patterns unflattering when they were transcribed and were concerned that they be 'tidied-up' as print. Others felt that their words conveyed their meanings inadequately or inaccurately. As one teacher said, 'I know you know what I meant, but outsiders might not'. It became important to re-emphasise that participants still controlled what they had said.

Once it was apparent that the researcher's response to a participant's misgivings was to make adjustments, clearing became a very positive act which improved a case study. Valuable new insights were offered into situations which had been only partially perceived in field notes. For example it was particularly helpful to gather additional perceptions of staff meetings described. When adjustments were appropriate they produced a more accurate picture. Because the researcher was offering his perceptions, participants were willing to respond with further insights. In one instance, the perception that difficult decisions over industrial action had been negotiated without rancour prompted staff to explain the detailed informal mechanisms by which this had been achieved.

Case study insights were often confirmed. 'That's very important'. 'I can remember it as clearly as if it were yesterday'. But the time gap between observing and clearance was particularly illuminating when changes had occurred. Comments such as 'You wouldn't recognise the staffroom now;' 'That's changed now,' were confirmatory evidence for developing hypotheses on how schools change. For example, it was fascinating to hear how a new member's arrival at a critical developmental phase in one school's staff relationships had acted as a catalyst which accelerated openness. A welfare assistant's account of how she had now 'learned the language' of the staff reinforced understanding of assimilation to staff membership: 'When someone says we're painting this afternoon, I think "Right, we'll need newspaper on those tables and the paints out and the aprons and so on". Whereas I used to think, "Oh, that's nice"'.

Implicit in the research structure of using interviews to collect multiple perceptions of the same situation was the knowledge that each of us is the centre of our own universe. We evaluate all information from that stance. But this knowledge was vividly confirmed when staff were given the full case study to read. As Ball (1982, p. 19) had found, sometimes 'The staff responded from their particular view of the school from the vantage point of the position they held'. Although staff members had cleared extracts individually, seeing them as part of a full case study was akin to seeing them in a new context. For us as researchers the case studies were documents constructed to give a picture of a year in the life of a whole primary school, with a research agenda in mind, seeking to incorporate the perspectives of those we observed. For members of the school the picture was also a biographical extract from their individual professional and personal lives. Our lens sometimes responded differently from their individual lenses. As researchers we would 'zoom-in' on incidents whose significance was in their research implications. The link between a series of 'close-ups' might be the pattern of interaction they illustrated for a researcher. But participants were concerned as much with the personal implications of the content of interaction as with interaction processes. As researchers we allowed for considerations of self-presentation when deciding what observation and interview extracts were appropriate to use, knowing what 'When an individual plays a part he implicitly requests his observers to take seriously the impression that is fostered before them' (Goffman, 1959, p.28). But as the centre of a different universe the researcher's insight into what would and would not be sensitive was bound to be partial. Individual participants sometimes 'zoomed in' according to when and how they participated. Natural concern for self-presentation could generate new significant links in the mind of a participant. These might be non-material in research terms but could have important meanings from an individual participant perspective. Thus negotiation at this stage meant responding to individual sensitivity.

Clearance produced changes in case study detail but not in case study structure. Though there was apprehension that some vital element might disappear, the negotiation experience suggests clearance as a positive phase which contributes to the richness of a case study. Clearance validates, corrects and extends insights. A unique perception becomes a joint one. Each staff's cohesion and each member's self-image can be safeguarded without compromising research.

There are clearance bonuses. Though the project was not conceived primarily as action research, several participants have said that involvement in the research has changed the way they approach the experience of leading and belonging to a school staff — confirmation that the lens is well-directed.

❑ References

Ball, S.J. (1982) 'Beachside considered: reflections on a methodological apprenticeship'. Conference paper, Whitelands College, London.

Goffman, E. (1971) *The Presentation of Self in Everyday Life*, Harmondsworth: Penguin.

Hammersley, M. and Atkinson, P. (1983) *Ethnography: Principles in Practice*, London: Tavistock Publications.

 Reading 12

The Use of Documentation to Check on Interview Data

Johnson, D. (1993), *Using Documents to Check on Interview Data*

(A retrospective account, specially commissioned for this volume of documentary research which formed part of Johnson's Leverhulme funded study 'The Coexistence of Public and Private Education', 1983–5)

To explore the effect of the existence of private sector institutions on the supply of students to maintained colleges of further and higher education, I interviewed a number of senior staff in such colleges. At that time (1984/5) their student records were not computerised. The colleges were not seriously addressing the market of school-leavers or sixth formers from independent schools, but reported their subjective impression that on certain courses between 10 per cent and 20 per cent of students had previously been privately educated. To check on this somewhat vague impression, with the help of a research assistant I invested several research days in making a manual check of 3,000 record cards of students on their relevant courses, to establish which schools they had previously attended.

Most of the cards were held in the central administration offices, but in some cases my assistant and I had to rummage in cupboards to find boxes of the relevant data. In Scott's (1990) terms, the *representativeness* of the data may have been dubious, in that there may have been further boxes which we did not find. There seemed little doubt about the *authenticity* of the data. Although we were not looking at students' original application forms, there was no reason why it would be in the interests of administrative staff to falsify their entries of the schools or colleges previously attended by students. Our main investigative problem in fact proved to be that administrative staff had *no* interest in this information, and had recorded it in the briefest possible fashion, giving only the name of the school or college and its town of location. Here was a clear example of documents prepared with a different purpose in mind from the purpose of the researchers using them.

To ascertain whether the schools listed on the records had, in each case, been independent, county or voluntary aided, proved a laborious task. Except where local knowledge made this unnecessary for us, we checked each school or college individually in the Education Authorities' Directory and all the relevant Almanacks for independent schools. Some students had had a chequered career, moving from school to school, and in many cases beginning their education overseas. We had to make the decision to refer only to the most recent school or college attended before enrolment at the college whose records we were checking.

As our work proceeded, we were increasingly challenged by its difficulty, and became more and more inventive in discovering sources of information about particularly elusive schools named. Eventually we were able to categorise almost all the previous schools attended, and collate our 'results' which we fed back to the colleges concerned. Nine years later, I no longer have the tables we compiled, but the research effort was reported and summarised in this chapter note to my book *Private Schools and State Schools* (1987, p.157):

> As a check against heads of departments' subjective impressions that between 10 and 20 per cent of full-time students on certain courses had previously been educated in the private sector, the records of 3,000 students were examined to establish where they had received their secondary education. For the years and the courses in question, the percentage of enroled students who had previously attended private schools was for some courses substantially lower and for others substantially higher than the heads of departments had estimated.

The colleges were not only not addressing the private sector as a market, but at that time they evidently had no accurate perception of the educational origins of the students they enrolled.

As an aspect of research enquiry, the rather tedious activity of checking student records which I have described comes under the heading of 'triangulation'. By examining research evidence from different points of view, the hope is that different sorts of data will point to the same findings, and reinforce the conclusions drawn.

In the example I have given, the study of records did not in fact reinforce college lecturers' fairly confident statements in interview that they knew the percentage of students joining the college from the private sector. It did however reinforce my own impression that these statements by lecturers were based on extremely slender knowledge of the schools and colleges, both public and private, from which their student body was drawn at that time.

For the research student, the main point is that a single source of data must always be to some extent suspect, and that every effort must be made, with the research resources available, to check the accuracy of data by using a combination of research tools.

❏ References

Johnson, D. (1987) *Private Schools and State Schools: Two Systems or One?* Milton Keynes: Open University Press.

Scott, J. (1990) *A Matter of Record,* Cambridge: Polity Press.

 **Reading 13**

Negotiation of Access for Observation

Hilsum, S. and Kane, B.S. (1971) *The Teacher's Day*, Windsor: NFER. pp. 23–25

[...] We concluded that it was the teacher rather than the pupils about whom we should be concerned. Pupil 'abnormality' soon disappeared once the novelty of the observer's presence had faded; most teachers, however, would only feel relaxed and 'normal' if they sensed that the observer's presence constituted no threat of any kind, either to their own position or to their relationship with their pupils. Our aim, therefore, was to reassure the teacher so that he became unperturbed by, and even indifferent to, the observer's presence — we wanted to achieve a situation where, in fact, the teacher simply forgot that he was being observed.

The procedure we adopted was a follows: the project was explained first to the representatives of the several county associations of heads and teachers, and an advisory committee was formed. Eleven separate meetings were then held in different parts of the county, and all primary heads in the country were invited to attend any of these; at these meetings we outlined the project and answered any question put to us. With the permission of the heads concerned, we then visited all the 66 sampled schools, and in each school we introduced ourselves to the two teachers who had been sampled. We explained that all records obtained would remain anonymous and that our observations contained no element of judgement about the teachers' methods or attitudes. We tried to make them thoroughly familiar with the procedures and aims of the research; we encouraged them to ask any questions or make any comments about what was involved. At that point the teachers were asked if we could arrange an 'acceptance visit' for each of them.[1]

On an 'acceptance day', the observer attended at the school for a whole day and gave the teacher and his pupils a chance to familiarize themselves with the whole observing and recording procedure, including the use of the radio-microphone. Samples of the teacher's work were recorded and shown to the teacher if he wished to see them. (These were intended only as 'practice' samples; none were used in our analysis). At breaks and lunch-time the teacher was again encouraged to ask any questions, and the out-of-school diary schedules were explained to him. The acceptance day also provided the observer with an opportunity to acquaint himself with the classroom and school situation and, through their conversations during the day, the teacher and observer could develop a relaxed relationship. (It was understood, of course, that on the 'real' observation days, the observer would become a spectator, divorced from the situation. There would be no observer-teacher or observer-pupil interaction, apart from the normal civilities of a 'Good morning', etc).

During the preliminary conversations, some teachers declared themselves already contented about the position and said they did not require an acceptance visit; others, during the course of the acceptance day, said they were satisfied and it was not necessary for the observer to stay for the full day. However, we always tried to keep to our arranged procedure, partly to make sure we were seen by other pupils and staff, for they also had to accept us around the school and in the staffroom. We regarded one acceptance day as a minimum acclimatization period; we always offered to return for another if the teacher had any doubts about his or the pupils' 'normality', but no teacher who had experienced the acceptance visit said he needed a second.

At the end of the acceptance day, the teacher was asked if he would participate in the project.[2] The careful introduction for the teacher had ensured that each participant had the maximum opportunity to assuage his doubts, to get his queries answered, and to gain confidence both in the observer as a person and in the procedure or recording. We felt that this part of the project was much appreciated by the teachers, to the extent that, of 141 teachers approached, 132 agreed to participate.[3] This degree of response, in our opinion, was an indication that the teachers had accepted in a positive way the notion of having an observer in the classroom, i.e. their anxieties or feelings of insecurity had been dispelled; this had been the objective of the whole preparatory exercise, for it was the teachers' anxieties, we believed, that might have made the observed classroom situations 'abnormal'.

We were satisfied, then, that the element of 'abnormality' in the observed situation had been reduced to a minimum; that when the actual observation day arrived, the classroom situation would be almost completely unaffected by the presence of the observer. However, we wished to test our belief. Accordingly, at the end of the actual observation day, the teacher was asked if, and to what extent, he believed he himself or the pupils had been affected by the observer's presence. This issue is discussed in further detail, but we can say here that the conclusion of our feasibility study, viz. that if our procedure was followed, then the classroom situation would be altered very little, was substantially confirmed.[4]

One point about the observation procedure remains to be mentioned, and it is most important with regard to the credence the reader will give to our findings. In order to remove any suggestion of 'preparation' on the part of the teachers, we did not give any advance notice to either heads or teachers of the actual days on which we would visit schools for the sampled observation visits. The observer just arrived at the school about 8.45 a.m. without warning, and recorded the day as he found it. The teachers who agreed to take part knew that this would be the method of proceeding, although they also understood from our discussions with them that there was to be no 'judgement' of their work and no advantage would be gained for them or for the project if they modified their day to impress the observer.

[...]

Figure A.II.5 *Completed specimen of teacher's out-of-school recording schedule*

| School: | 4 | Day: | FRIDAY |
| Teacher: | B | Date: | 31.1.69 |

Activity	Total Time (in mins)
MARKING AND ASSESSING e.g. marking ex. books, exams, tests, writing reports for Head, parents, probation officer, other schools; making assessments for school record cards, reports.	35
LESSON PLANNING e.g. referring to text books, making notes; estimating equipment required; writing, referring to record/ forecast of work.	40
STAFF MEETING	nil
OTHER MEETINGS e.g. attending PTA; Professional Association Meeting; School Sports Association.	nil
SPECIAL OCCASION e.g. Open Day; Sports Day; Speech Day; Jumble Sale; School social occasion, School concert, play.	nil
SCHOOL VISITS e.g. taking pupils on school visit, trip.	nil

PROFESSIONAL COURSE/READING e.g. reading for background information, further qualifications; professional journal; attending course, conference on professional matters.	15
CLUB ACTIVITIES e.g. attending, organising football, netball fixture (home or away); games practice; chess, orchestra, drama.	nil
ADMINISTRATION e.g. (excluding club activities) estimating stock requirements; planning timetable; planning, organising school outing; making duty roster.	nil
RECORDING e.g. copying, calling out list of names, marks; counting money; copying information into reports or records; totalling registers.	nil
EQUIPMENT e.g. making equipment; moving equipment; giving out, collecting equipment (inc. books); tidying, clearing up desks, room; searching for equipment.	25
PUPIL WELFARE e.g. speaking to parents, pupil(s) about home, personal interests; dealing with pupils' private property, dealing with pupil(s) who is (are) unwell.	nil
DIRECT TUITION e.g. instructing, demonstrating; marking with pupil; listening, watching (with class) radio, T.V., visiting speaker.	nil
SUPERVISION/PATROL e.g. patrolling building, playground; coach escort; detention. a) when on duty; b) when not on duty;	a) nil b) nil
TALKING TO ADULTS e.g. other teachers (inc. Head), secretary, cook, caretaker, dinner helpers, student, visitors (e.g. medical, organiser), classroom ancillary.	10
INVIGILATING EXAMS e.g. LEA or other external tests.	nil
EVENING CLASS e.g. teaching at night school; supervising youth club.	nil
OTHER (please specify)	

❑ Notes

1. We have summarized the 'approach' procedure here. The reader is referred to Appendix I for further details and discussion.

2. This is an important point. The teachers were randomly selected and then asked to volunteer; thus the research procedure ensured that no suggestion could be made to the effect that the sample of teachers consisted of 'special' teachers.

3. Some of the refusals were concerned with the teacher's ill-health, the remainder with hostility to the project. All refusals occurred during early discussions, well before the matter of an acceptance visit could be raised.

4. Oddly enough, although in the previous literature this matter of abnormality resulting from an observer's presence is discussed at some length, the only attempt to gauge some measure of the observer's effect was made during the study by Stukat (1967).

South East Essex College
of Arts & Technology
Carnarvon Road Southend-on-Sea Essex SS2 6LS
Tel: (01702) 220400 Fax: (01702) 432320 Minicom: (01702) 220642

 **Reading 14**

Planning Your Research Project — The Single-handed Researcher

Johnson, D. (1984) 'Planning small-scale research' in Bell, S. et al. (Eds) *Conducting Small-Scale Investigations in Educational Management*, London: Harper and Row, pp. 5–18

[...]

❑ The stages of carrying out an investigation

The inexperienced investigator, faced with the need to 'do some research' as part of a course of study or to give a wider perspective to personal experience, may welcome the security of a list by which to order the research activity. The following has been found useful in classifying the stages of activity which must be worked through in carrying out and completing an investigation.

1. Establishing the focus of the study
2. Identifying the specific objectives of the study
3. Selecting the research method
4. Arranging research access
5. Developing the research instrument
6. Collecting the data
7. Pulling out of the investigative phase
8. Ordering of the data
9. Analysing the data
10. Writing up
11. Enabling dissemination

Each stage will be discussed in turn, bearing in mind that the investigation in question is likely to be small scale. Most of the examples used will be drawn from educational research, and the assumption will be made that the investigation is being undertaken as a means to a particular end (of academic qualification or occupational advancement) rather than as part of a continuing and professional research career.

1. Establishing the focus of the study

When students are questioned about a preferred subject for a mini-project or research-based dissertation, they may say 'I'd like to do something about

Saturday schools', or 'I've always been interested in pastoral care'. They are halfway towards deciding on the general area for their study, but have many more questions to ask themselves before they have established its focus. Are they interested in examining Saturday schools as institutions for the perpetuation and promotion of particular cultures (in which case they might want to look at Polish schools and Hebrew schools, as well as the more recently established Saturday schools for Asian or West Indian children)? Or are they interested to establish the part played by parents in the setting up and resourcing of a Saturday school? In this case examples of recently established schools would give better access to memory and documentation than would a long-running school, the contributions of whose founding fathers and mothers have been overlaid by the sediment of rules and traditions. Does the student interested in pastoral care want to investigate it in terms of its implications for the career patterns of teachers? Or perhaps as an example of the cross-fertilization of ideas between the independent and maintained schools? Or in terms of the use of a pastoral care system to identify and help withdrawn pupils? All of these ideas, and many more, may be in the background of a student's 'interest' in a topic, but they cannot all form the subject of the same investigation.

It is true that, when set down in words, the focused subject of an investigation may sound as dry as dust. This is probably why so many dissertation, these and project have sub-titles, explaining the scope of the study, but preceded by a more eye-catching and evocative main title. For example:

School closure — A study of changes in governing body membership and activity during a programme of secondary school closures in one local authority

The sub-title makes it plain what the investigator has set out to do, and what kind of information the reader can expect to be given. The overall title reassures them both that the investigation contributes to understanding of an important social phenomenon, and that this wider context is not forgotten in the account given of the investigation.

It is not until the investigator has so concentrated the subject of the study that it can be expressed in one sentence, that he or she can be said to have established the focus of the investigation and be ready to move to the next stage.

2. Identifying the specific objectives of the study
The cynical investigator's approach to the setting of specific objectives is to 'wait until you have finished, see what you've managed to achieve, then say

this was your objective'. Whilst it is to be hoped that this practice is rarely followed in any wholesale way, some minor *post hoc* modification of objectives probably contributes to the cut-and-dried tidiness of many a research account.

But the attempt to define specific objectives in advance should not be abandoned for fear they will not, in the event, be met. Identifying particular objectives helps the investigator along the road to choosing the research method and deciding on the forms of access needed, and may contribute to the selection and development of a suitable research instrument.

The background reading, or review of the literature, which is an essential contextual element of any piece of research, will ideally take place at this stage, so that it can influence the formation of research objectives. In practice, literature relevant to the subject of investigation may prove to be scanty, or may only be identified later in the research.

If the investigator has a particular personal interest in, and commitment to, the subject of study, one way to identify specific objectives is to ask 'What will I be disappointed not to have learned (or had experience of) once the study is over?' For example, in a study of home-school relations the researchers were particularly eager to learn how secondary schools were viewed from the point of view of the home, to complement the many accounts of home-school relations given from the point of view of the school. One of the specific objectives of the study was, therefore to recruit parental opinion, and to do this away from the milieu of the school. In fieldwork terms, this meant devoting nearly all the resources of the project to setting up and carrying out home interviews with parents. But meeting this particular objective of recruiting parental opinion also satisfied the researchers that they had not missed the opportunity to explore an aspect of home-school relations which they held to be neglected in other accounts (Johnson and Ransom, 1983).

If the researcher's approach to the subject of study is a more detached one, with little sense of personal involvement or commitment (as is probably most frequently the case with the kind of 'means-to-an-end' investigation discussed in this paper) the identification of specific objectives may seem more arbitrary. But it will still help towards later stages of the study by highlighting particular fieldwork needs. For example, the investigator planning to make the study of school closure in terms of its implications for the relevant school governing bodies, might set the specific objectives of including pupil governors in the range of members interviewed. Or, in a study of the role of head teachers of comprehensive schools, an investigator might set the objective of including an equal number of headmistresses and headmasters in the enquiry. (Such an objective would have implications for the geographical scope of the investigation, since headmistresses are more thinly spread across the secondary school system than are headmasters).

3. Selecting the research method

This is the next stage in planning the study. Ideally the research method should not be decided until the focus and objectives of the investigation are clear. In practice, professional researchers tend to prefer those methods of investigation in which they have a cumulative expertise, and will tailor the subject of study to make possible the use of their well-tried research techniques. Inexperienced or self-supporting researchers may also feel tempted to decide on a research method before giving detailed consideration to the subject of their investigation. The requirements of their course of study, or the sparsity of research resources may, in fact, rule out the use of certain methods such as, for example, some of the 'unobtrusive measures' discussed by Webb et al. (1966) which have to be recorded over a lengthy period. Nevertheless, the selection of the research method is a crucial element in the planning of an investigation. A range of possible methods and some guidelines for choosing between them are discussed in a later section of this paper.

4. Arranging research access

If an entirely quantitative method is to be used, such as the issue of a postal questionnaire, the notion of arranging research access may seem superfluous. People cannot prevent the post being delivered to their home or place of work. Nevertheless, even in such a case the investigator must give thought to what can be done to improve the receptivity of the addressee to the questionnaire, and hence increase the likelihood that he or she will complete and return it. In one way or another the envelope, covering letter and questionnaire itself must perform the tasks which the investigator might otherwise carry out in person, when arranging research access. These tasks can be summarized as:

(a) imparting the conviction that the investigation is a worthwhile piece of work and the investigator a competent person to carry it out
(b) explaining why the investigation seeks the cooperation of the person or institutions being approached
(c) indicating the use to be made of the eventual research material

In the case of educational research the negotiation of research access if unlikely to be a once-and-for-all event. The investigator must be prepared to reiterate, to a succession of audiences, the purposes, style, scope and utility of the proposed research, and these explanations may have to be communicated in a number of different ways. For example, to make a study of secondary school responses to the behaviour of disaffected pupils (Bird et al. 1981), getting research access entailed formal correspondence with selected chief education officers, meetings at local authority offices with particular head teachers, debate (and defence) of the proposed research in the staff rooms of their schools, and face-to-face assurances regarding the scope and confidentiality of the research to individual teachers and pupils who were asked to take part. This was a sizeable piece of research involving four researchers, and on a sensitive topic. However, the investigator whose chosen sphere is education is likely to find that almost any topic is deemed 'sensitive' by some of those asked to take part.

In setting up a single-handed study within the confines of one's own school or college, as many teacher-investigators are likely to do, there will still be a need to get the formal agreement of the headteacher and relevant heads of departments, and the active cooperation of any teachers, ancillary staff or pupils whose help is required. Depending on the subject of study, the headteacher may consider that the approval of parents must also be sought, and it is to be hoped that he or she will agree to obtain this by telephone or letter, on behalf of the investigator.

If documentary research is being undertaken, and the access required is to files and papers rather than individuals or situations, then it is with the keepers of the archives in question that access must be arranged.

Whatever the research method being used, the investigator will find that agreement to research access must be kept in good repair throughout the enquiry. Even if agreement has been given, the careless or off-hand investigator may become *persona non grata* during the course of the research, and be unable to complete it. If files are left in disarray, papers borrowed and not returned, or respondents subjected to too lengthy or frequent interviews, at inconvenient times, the researcher's welcome will be worn out. All social researchers are to some extent mendicants, since they are seeking a free gift of time or information from those who are subject of study. But researchers who bear this fact in mind, and who, without becoming the captive of their respondents, can contrive to make the research experience a helpful and profitable one, will almost certainly be gratified by the generosity with which people will give their time and knowledge.

5. Developing the research instrument

The research instrument may be an interview schedule or a postal question-naire. Or it may be a set of guidelines for an unstructured interview, or a pro forma for the classification of information selected from records. In some cases, the research instrument may be the trained capacity of an individual to make notes about the circumstances and content of a meeting. (A tape recorder, it should be stressed is *not* a research instrument. It is simply a means of enabling the reiteration of audible material in a place and at a time other than when it was recorded. The researcher's essential task of selection from and analysis of that material still remains to be done.)

The important point about research instruments is that they require development — they do not spring to hand in a perfect form, fully adapted to the particular investigative task. All formal texts on research methods mentioned the desirability of a 'pilot study', and this is one way in which a research instrument can be honed to its particular task. Trying out an interview schedule on a sample of respondents with similar characteristics to those of the intended survey population, for example, may quickly reveal gaps in the logical sequence of questions, or the incomprehensibility to the respondent of the wording used. 'I had no idea a Rising Five was a child', said one school governor. 'I thought it was something to do with fishing tackle'.

The luxury of a genuine pilot study, which tries out in miniature the viability of an envisaged investigation, is unlikely to be available to the student planning a small-scale short-term piece of research. But at least some attempt at 'trying it on the dog' should be made. Questionnaires and interview schedules in particular must be tried out on *someone* — friends, relations, neighbours. The investigator will get valuable feedback, for example, on whether 'closed' questions can readily be answered in the terms of the suggested range of replies.

Experience will be gained of how long it will take a respondent to fill in the questionnaire, or for an interview schedule to be worked through — important information for the overall planning of the investigation. Such *ad hoc* trials will confirm the need for any questionnaire or schedule to go through several draft stages, the number of which will depend on the time available.

In the case of a pro forma for recording information extracted from files, for example pupil records, the design of such a tool may have had to take place without prior knowledge of the range of information likely to be available. Teachers researching in their own institution will be more fortunate here, as they will have some notion of what is usually recorded. But if access is negotiated to the pupil records of *another* school, the range of information available may be different again, and the pro forma has to be rapidly adapted. Complete redesign may be needed in some cases, and it is to be hoped that the files can be studied on more than one occasion.

It can be seen that development of the research instrument may take place either before or during its use. Where the instrument is the researcher's own capacity to observe and record, this will certainly develop in the course of research experience. However, short-term small-scale investigations may provide only brief opportunities for 'learning on the job'. The investigator should do everything possible to prepare for the event to be observed. For example, in the case of a meeting the observer should try to sort out the names and roles of those present before the meeting starts or, if this is impossible, at least note some identifying physical characteristic of each person, and where they are sitting in relation to others. After the event, whether it be a case conference or a governing body meeting, a helpful informant may then be prepared to help the observer discover the identify and contribution of each person.

One factor influencing the eventual form of any research instrument must be the form of analysis which is to be applied to the data after they have been collected. For example, the tables it is intended to draw up using collated information from questionnaires or schedules, should be decided on and listed at the time the research instrument is designed. If these decisions are left until after the fieldwork has been done, the investigator may find that a question vital to the analysis has not been asked. And although qualitative forms of investigation may be seen as exploratory, with the intention that any analytic theory shall be grounded in the research material which comes to hand during the fieldwork, interviews or observers should still, at this 'research instrument' stage, provide themselves with guidelines which ensure the coverage of what are likely to be the eventual analytic themes of the research account.

6. Collecting the data

Developing the research instrument may, as we have seen, lap over into data collection, but for many research designs the fieldwork period is a distinct and discrete phase of the investigation. Its clear demarcation may, in fact, be essential to the successful completion of the whole enquiry. This is the period during which the researcher is likely to be investing most in the study, by way of time and personal involvement. Marking out a definite period during which the fieldwork is to be pursued helps concentration and commitment to the task in hand, for the fieldwork period is one when other customary social or work activities may well have to be set aside, reduced or postponed.

What the fieldwork actually consists of will depend upon the research design. It may be interviewing, documentary study or observation — all are forms of data collection which, in a small-scale study, are likely to entail the personal involvement of the investigator. Only in the case of a postal questionnaire will there be a 'breather' for the researcher while the research instrument is in the field. In this particular case the pre- and post-fieldwork periods are likely to be the busiest, when the questionnaire is being designed and developed before its issue, and when the completed questionnaires are being studied after they are returned.

One problem for the researcher whose fieldwork takes the form of interviewing or observation is that the period set aside for fieldwork may, fortuitously, prove not to be a good time for the study of the social phenomenon he or she has set out to investigate. In social research there is rarely an opportunity for the use of a controlled experimental model. A social life is untidy and episodic, and although investigators may contrive to insert themselves into the milieux in which they are interested, during a given period there may be few opportunities to acquire data by the method planned. A Master's student investigating the education provided to adolescents in hospital for short-term treatment had as one objective the interviewing of such patients, as well as the study of the organizational infrastructure of hospital schooling (Smith, 1981). From the point of view of the investigator it was a disappointment that during the period allocated for fieldwork only a few patients within the eligible group were, in fact, admitted to the hospital under study. The student had to make the most of her small available sample — but also had to resist the temptation to extend the fieldwork period, in the hope that more patients would be admitted.

For not only must the research decided when to start the fieldwork, but a decision must also be made when to end it. This is the essence of the next stage to be discussed.

7. Pulling out of the investigative phase
Under this heading we can also discuss the whole question of 'getting away with the data', for the novice researcher may find it is just as difficult to pull out of a single interview as to say 'finis' to the fieldwork period as a whole.

To deal first with this problem of ending an interview, it is always the responsibility of the interviewer to do this, rather than waiting for the respondent to call a halt, however unstructured and relaxed the interview situation may be. It may have been difficult to negotiate access and to get in in the first place, but the interviewer who, once in, stays until he is thrown out, is working in the style of investigative journalism rather than social research.

Face-to-face interviewing evokes the conventions of normal polite social intercourse, and it is unethical and unfair to push the respondent into the position of breaking those conventions by saying he has had enough, when an interviewer outstays his welcome or his allotted time. The interviewer whose respondent says he can spare an hour should not outstay that period however much both parties may settle in to enjoying and profiting from the occasion, without formally raising the question of whether an extended discussion, or a second interview, would be desirable and feasible. If an interview takes two or three times as long as the interviewer said it would, the respondent, whose other work or social activities have been accordingly delayed, will be irritated in retrospect, however enjoyable the experience may have been at the time. This sort of practice breaks one of the ethics of professional social research, which is that the field should not be left more difficult for subsequent investigators to explore by disenchanting respondents with the whole notion of research participation.

There are other questions of more personal ethics to be borne in mind, when private interviews are being conducted. Respondents become vulnerable during the course of extended sympathetic interviewing, and if the interview is unduly prolonged may begin to say things they will subsequently regret or talk themselves into a despondent frame of mind, if the interview has focused on problems. The interviewer may feel increasingly unable to terminate the interview and leave the depressed respondent alone, and is in danger of losing professional control of the situation by stepping out of the role of social enquirer to become the confidant of the person being interviewed. The writer makes it a rule, for example when conducting home interviews with parents, not to leave respondents in a worse state than that in which she found them. This can mean keeping an eye on how time is passing and devoting part of the available period to winding-down conversation which diverts the respondent from problems discussed to more positive aspects of their life experience.

Difficulties of this kind may perhaps be unlikely to crop up in small-scale research in which fieldwork may well be confined to interaction with known colleagues. Nevertheless, the novice researcher should be alert to the possibilities that such difficulties may occur, and may perhaps be precipitated by overlong research contact with one individual. A problem which all will encounter, however, is the wider one of calling a halt to the investigative period as a whole.

Can the researcher be flexible about how long to wait for questionnaires to come back? Can use be made of those which come trailing in long after the rest? If a meeting which it was hoped to observe is postponed, should efforts be made to attend it when it is reconvened? If the target population proves thin on the ground during the period set aside for interview, can that period be extended? In the case of small-scale research, the answer to any of these questions must usually be 'No'. The fault from which many amateur investigations — and some professional ones — suffer is that of any open-ended period of data collection. Almost all social enquiries produce more data than can subsequently be made use of, however short the fieldwork period. And if this is endlessly extended, perhaps because the researcher has become fascinated with the phenomenon under study, there is a danger that none of the material may be adequately taken through the outstanding stages of the investigation. Research which is not completed is no research at all.

8. Ordering of the data

All research material, however collected, should be set in order and stored in a form in which it would be comprehensible to others, were they to be given access to it. Some kind of research archive or data bank must be established. However slender the data their sole repository must not be between the ears of the investigator, or a fundamental tenet of research — that the material must be testable and contestable by others — is not being met. Questionnaires and interview schedules must be collated and classified, field notes must be written up, and a reckoning should be kept of the timing and incidence of the fieldwork. Researchers must be prepared to be accountable for the investigations they have undertaken, even if they are never called to render that account.

A further reason for putting the data together in an orderly form is applicable both to large and small-scale research. The disorganized investigator is in danger of making disproportionate use of the more striking or memorable research material and neglecting to balance this with other more humdrum data. When moving to the task of analysis the totality of the acquired data needs to be surveyed.

9. Analysing the data

The main general point to be made about this stage is that it must exist and be allowed for in the overall research programme. An investigator should not move directly from data collection to writing up, however small-scale the study. A weakness of many dissertations or theses is that, although considerable pains may have been taken to set up and carry out an effective piece of fieldwork, little use is made of the data collected in the eventual discussion of the thesis topic. Instead, discussion appears to be chiefly based on the investigator's background reading and/or preconceived ideas about the subject of study. In such cases it is likely that the student has not allowed sufficient time to muse on and learn from the research material.

The broad analytic themes of the study will, as we have already indicated, have to be identified before embarking on the fieldwork. But the data collected must be drawn on to illuminate those themes, and may well call into question the research's implicit assumptions about the topic.

10. Writing up

This is perhaps the most difficult, but potentially the most satisfying, phase of the research. By putting words on paper about his research the investigator makes it available to other scholars and, in the classic phrase, pushes back the frontiers of knowledge, however minutely.

Technical advice on the format of research accounts if fairly readily available and cannot be included here. Important features are that the text shall be understandable and unambiguous, the referencing punctilious and accurate, and the overall conclusion or 'message' of the research be summarized in an assimilable and memorable form.

Writing up research can never be simply an exercise in handing on the data to the reader for his or her consideration. In a quantitative study tables may be compiled which, to the investigator, may seem self-explanatory, but some discussion of them must appear in the eventual text. In a qualitative study, quotations may be selected from the research material for inclusion in the research account, but these do not render superfluous a clear summative statement by the researcher of the beliefs or sentiments which the quotations serve to illustrate. The essence of an effective research account is that it conveys to the reader something of a researcher's empirical experience, together with his reflections on it.

11. Enabling dissemination

Although the active and continuing dissemination of research findings may not be a feasible part of a small-scale investigation, the investigator has a duty to make dissemination possible. Writing an account of the research may be all the investigator can do, but some thought should be given to the number and durability of copies of that account, and the formal and informal circulation of them which can be arranged or permitted.

Various methods exist by which the dissemination of research material can be agreed with those who participated in the enquiry. The nonconfidentiality of the materials may have been clearly accepted by participants from the outset, in which case no further negotiation is strictly necessary regarding the open circulation of the eventual research report. Nevertheless, it is courteous to supply a draft copy for comment to the principal 'gatekeeper' who allowed the research to go forward.

It has already been pointed out that almost all educational research is felt to be sensitive by some of those taking part. If individuals or institutions are to be named in the research account, explicit 'clearance' of the document by those concerned is desirable and advisable. Where anonymity has been required as a condition of the investigation, this should be scrupulously preserved by the use of pseudonyms and the editing of descriptive materials in such a way as to make identification of individuals or institutions at least difficult, if not impossible. This professional practice should not be regarded by the student investigator as unnecessary for a research account which 'no one will see'. The whole point of a research account is that someone other than the writer shall see it, and it may well prove of interest to a select or extended circle of researchers and/or educationalist.

By taking the trouble to meet the requirements of the research participants with regard to clearance or confidentiality, the investigator has made possible the wider dissemination of the research findings and given some protection to informants in the event of the account being circulated or reproduced without the researcher's permission. (Such practices, whilst undesirable, are not unknown.)

Verbal dissemination of research findings (supplementing, but never replacing, a written research account) may prove useful, and is perhaps especially desirable in the case of small-scale means-to-an-end research which does not lead to published work. Whilst it cannot be regarded as an essential stage of the research enquiry, the teacher-investigator may find it worthwhile to prepare a short list of key issues arising from his research which can form the basis of formal or informal discussion with colleagues or, where appropriate, pupils. Any other feasible form of dissemination should also be considered since, in addition to meeting the academic requirements of an enquiry, dissemination to some extent redresses the balance of researcher-participant indebtedness. By doing all he can to increase and disseminate understanding of the topic under study, the social enquirer is paying back something of what he has received by way of information and cooperation from his research participants.

[...]

❑ References

Bird, C., Chessum, R., Furlong, J. and Johnson, D. (Ed) (1981) *Disaffected Pupils*, Brunel University.

Johnson, D. and Ransom, E. (1983) *Family and School*, London, Croom Helm

Smith, J. (1981) 'An exploration of the schooling of pupils aged 13–16 who have to spend a short time in their local general hospital'. Unpublished dissertation, MA in Public and Social Administration, Department of Government, Brunel University.

Webb, E. J., Campbell, D. T., Schwartz, R.D. and Sechrest, L. (1966) *Unobtrusive Measures: Non-Reactive Research in the Social Sciences*, Chicago: Rand McNally.

Reading 15

The Literature Review I

Haywood, P and Wragg E.C. (1978) *Evaluating the Literature*, Rediguide 2, School of Education, Nottingham University, pp. 1–4

❏ Introduction

'You'd better find out what's been done first', is probably the most frequent supervisor response to the novice investigator convinced he has stumbled on some important unresearched issue. There is sometimes a case, perhaps, for not knowing what others have done in the field, and allowing untrammelled genius to canter through a research project. At its best this might produce refreshing new insights, at its worst exultant rediscovery of the wheel.

It is one thing to realise that a search of 'the literature' must be made, but quite another to know how and where to start. Many researchers with years of experience are unaware of the vast range of bibliographies, encyclopaedias, indexes and abstract services currently available. Several hours can be wasted searching for references which could be available in minutes if only the investigator know where to look.

Furthermore although reading of existing work in the field will inform you about other people's findings, commonly used research techniques, pitfalls, omissions and a host of other important matters which can enable you to make your own contribution much more effectively, novice researchers are sometimes very disappointed to discover that their inspired idea to investigate, say, the language, intellectual or social development of small children is already massively researched. A reading of published work in the field, however, might reveal that most investigators have looked at the role of the mother, but that far fewer have studied fathers. Further reading and reflection might identify an important, if relatively narrow, area where even a first-time researcher can try to make useful inroads.

❏ 1. A 'critical' review

The first time a third-year pupil is asked to write a 'critical account' of a poem, a play or a book he will almost certainly interpret the word 'critical' in its popular sense and argue that the work in question is dreadful. It is not unknown for this to occur at a more advanced level, and it is disappointing to read a research report which begins with a massive castigation of all previous enquiries, suggesting that the writer alone is a shining beacon of common sense, integrity and imagination, and then find his own research is even more excruciatingly banal, ill-conceived or sloppily executed than that of the hapless crew he has calumniated.

More frequent, however, is the *uncritical* review, the furniture sale catalogue, in which everything merits a one paragraph entry no matter how skilfully it has been conducted: Bloggs (1975) found this, Smith (1976) found that, Jones (1977) found the other, Bloggs, Smith and Jones (1978) found happiness in heaven.

A *critical* review should show that the writer has studied existing work in the field with insight. Consequently one finds phrases such as 'despite the smallness of the sample there was an intensive scrutiny of ..., in view of the low reliability of Factor E in the test used this result should be interpreted with caution, extraneous variables were much more effectively controlled in this study than the previous one', and 'as no replication of his work has ever approached the high correlations of the initial investigations...'. On the other hand you should not invent criticisms for window dressing or accept uncritically the approval or condemnation of certain pieces of work by others who have reviewed the field. Many people who read research reports are extremely knowledgeable in the field and recognise borrowed interpretation or pseudo critiques when they see them.

❑ 2. The need to be systematic

It is most important that you should undertake a review of the literature in a systematic way. It is rare for someone to find that they consult fewer than 30 books, articles or reports, and more likely that at the end of the day anything from 50 to 500 separate sources may have been either read intensively or skimmed through. Although in the first instance it is easy to remember where one saw a piece of information, or to keep notes on a motley collection of pieces of paper of varying size and colour, old envelopes and cards, it becomes increasingly inefficient and time-consuming.

One good idea is to keep a proper card index. You can buy lined cards of various sizes and keep them together. Many people find 8" x 5" a useful size. At the top the full bibliographical details need to be recorded: author's name and initials, title, publisher, city, date, page numbers, journal volume number, editor's name and initials if appropriate etc. One day you may have to list a bibliography in alphabetical order and, finding you never recorded page numbers, author's initials or the date of a book, you can waste hours seeking these out, sometimes having to wait for a book to be re-ordered on inter-library loan. An example of a card with the appropriate bibliographical details entered is shown in Figure 15.1.

KERLINGER, F.N.   1973

Foundations of Behavioural Research
(second edition)

New York, Hote, Rinehart & Winston

[has new chapters on multiple regulation]

Index   research design, statistics, regression
Card   R102

Figure 15.1

On the rest of the card, and on supplementary cards if necessary, you can preserve notes made whilst reading the book or article in question. Again it is worth making sure these are *accurate*, otherwise you may have to send for the book again merely to check the page number and wording of a quotation you wish to use. Record any data, tables or conclusions which seem relevant, and include any critical remarks, both of approval and disapproval, you may wish to make when writing your own review of the field. It is very difficult to recall all these merely from memory when several sources have been consulted.

This kind of systematisation will also make it easier to group studies when you are writing your review. It is much easier to read a research report when some attempt has been made to conceptualise the field under headings like 'teacher's role', 'personality' or 'home background', even if all the work referred to cannot be fitted in under such labels.

Finally be warned that 'systematic' is not a euphemism for 'overkill'. One of the problems faced by an investigator who is conscientious in his approach is that every new lead opens up a whole field in which there might be hundreds of books and articles. There is almost no topic in education which does not, before long, raise countless related issues to do with social class, personality, values, intellectual capacity, race, curriculum, history or politics. No-one can review each of these fields or be expected to be thoroughly expert in them. You must made the judgement about which hares to chase. Place most of your effort into reading about research which is central to your own areas of concern. Try also to make judicious choices about which pieces of research to record in most detail. If a report is well conceived and close to your own topic read it and record fully and carefully. If it is badly executed or peripheral, skim quickly and record more briefly, but making careful note of any weaknesses you have detected in it.

❑ 3. Building up a bibliography

At the beginning of an enquiry, particularly for anyone relatively new to the field, building up a bibliography and reading around an area can be a formidable task. There are usually more studies in the field than one suspects, often buried in thesis collections or less well know periodicals. English Language accounts include sometimes colossal numbers of American or Canadian work, as well as Australian, New Zealand, Indian and even African research. There are also translations of relevant Scandinavian or Russian studies. Consequently the advice of a good librarian should be sought at difficult stages in the search. Remember too that some sources may be in microfiche form, so this section of the catalogue should also be consulted.

[...]

 **Reading 16**

The Literature Review II

Lofthouse, M.T. and Whiteside, T.

Any investigation, whatever the scale, will involve reading what other people have written about your area of interest.

❏ What is a literature review?

A literature review interprets and synthesizes what has been researched and published in the area of interest. It should present the state of the art with regard to a certain topic. Such reviews usually assess the work to date and may even offer suggestions for future inquiry.

Depending on the problem, literature reviews can be characterised as primarily integrative, theoretical or methodological.

- *Integrative reviews* summarise past research
- *Theoretical reviews* focus on relevant theories
- *Methodological reviews* concentrate on research methods and definitions

In practice, most reviews integrate all relevant information on a topic, whether the information is from previous investigations, theory or methodology.

The literature is of two types

data-based research studies refers to studies that involve the collection and analysis of data gathered from people, organizations, documents etc.

non-data-based writings writer's experiences or opinions and can range from the highly theoretical to enthusiastic practitioner accounts

The amount of each type of literature will vary according to the problem. There will be many data-based studies on the topic of participation in adult education whereas most of the literature on theories of adult learning is likely to be conceptual and therefore non-data-based.

❑ Why do a literature review?

The most important reason for undertaking a literature review is to allow the researcher to reach the frontiers of knowledge in their particular problem area. Until you have learned what others have done in your area, you cannot develop a research project that will contribute to furthering knowledge in your field. Thus the literature in any field forms the foundation on which any future work should be built. If you fail to build this foundation of knowledge provided by the review of the literature, your work is likely to be shallow and naive, and will often duplicate work that has already been done better by someone else.

Undertaking the literature review will also allow you to identify the contribution made by your study to the knowledge base. It should help you in interpreting and analysing the evidence/data you have collected by allowing you to see how your study deviates from what has already been done. The question of how the present study advances, refines or revises what is already known is considerably more easy to answer when the researcher has undertaken a good critical literature review.

The literature review can also help in

- **Delimiting the research problem** The review of the literature can help in limiting the individual's research problem and in defining it better. It is far better in research to select a limited problem and treat it well rather than to attempt the study of a broad general problem and do it poorly.

- **Seeking new approaches** In the process of reviewing the literature, the student should not only learn what work has been done but also be alert to research possibilities that have been overlooked. The researcher's background and experience may allow them to see facets of the problem not seen by other research workers. Such new viewpoints are likely to occur most frequently in areas where little research has been done.

- **Avoiding sterile approaches** In reviewing the literature, the student should be on the look-out for research approaches to their problem that have proved to be sterile.

- **Insight into methods** The process of undertaking a literature review can contribute to answering specific design questions. Knowing what hypotheses have been advanced and tested previously, how terms have been defined, and what assumptions have been dealt with by other investigators can simplify the researcher's tasks.

- **Recommendations for further research** Authors of articles often include specific suggestions and recommendations for people planning further research in the field.

❏ When do you undertake a literature review?

Determining the best time to undertake a literature review is a matter for debate.

A literature review's impact on problem formulation is an interactive process. At one end of the continuum is reviewing the literature to find a problem; at the other end of the scale is reviewing the literature to see if the investigator's problem has ever been studied. Somewhere in the middle we find the investigator who has some notion about the research area and consults the literature for help in focusing the problem.

In small scale research it is likely that the bulk of your reading will come early in the investigation, though in practice a number of activities are generally in progress at the same time and reading may even spill over into the data collection stage of the study.

You must take care that reading does not take up too much time. There is a danger that you feel you must read the very latest book or search for another article. Make sure that apart from books and articles you have had difficulty in obtaining that you set a deadline for the reading stage.

❏ How do you conduct a literature review?

The steps involved

1. Search for literature that might be selected for review. The scope of the search will be determined by how well defined your research problem is, as well as by one's own familiarity with the topic. If you have only a vague sense of the topic examine books such as education encyclopaedias, handbooks etc. The next step is to check bibliographies, indexes and abstracts that reference specific aspects of a topic. this step in the search will be done by hand and by computer.

2. Decide which resources should be obtained and then which resources to include in the review. The selection can be made on the basis of the following criteria:
   - Is the author of the source an authority on the topic — one who has done much of the empirical work in the area or one who has

offered seminal theory upon which subsequent research and writing is based? If so, that author's work will be quoted by others and listed in the bibliographies on the topic.

- When was the article or book or report written? As a rule, the most recent work in an area should be included in the review.

- What exactly was written about or tested? If a particular resource or research study is highly relevant to your present research interest, it should be included even if the 'who' and 'when' criteria are not met.

- What is the quality of the source? A thoughtful analysis, a well-designed study, or an original way of viewing the topic is probably a significant piece of literature.

Knowing when to stop reviewing the literature is as important as knowing where and how to locate sources. A sense of being saturated signals the end of the search. When you begin to encounter familiar references and have stopped finding significant new resources, it is time to quit.

❑ What makes for a quality literature review?

Reviews should be critical. They should provide the reader with a picture of the state of knowledge and of major questions in the subject area being investigated. It should read as a synthesis, written by someone who has read all of the literature and so is able to look across it all, select the highlights and synthesize these into a totally integrated section.

A review of the literature is different from annotated bibliography which consists of a series of independent references to single studies. If we read over our review of the literature and each paragraph refers to a different specific study or reference, then we have not achieved this integration function sufficiently well.

In writing the reveiw we should remember that

- Being 'critical' does not mean that you have to show that all previous work was dreadful or misguided. It should show that the writer has studied existing work in the field with insight.

- it is not necessary to include within the review all the literature that you have read. The selection of what is to be reviewed should be made in terms of what is relevant and necessary to understand the study. Reading that was useful in providing background information but is not needed to understand the present study can and should be eliminated. The bibliography can if necessary include a list of all the texts consulted by the author.

- the goal is to review the literature in the context of our study. 'Thus each point made and each reference cited should be written in such a way that the reader sees its relevance to, and contribution in establishing, the foundation for the current study' (Fox, 1969, p. 726).

- 'we are writing the review of the literature for our future use when we write the discussion of our results and conclusions from our study. In those later chapters we will want to refer to the findings of our previous studies and the conclusions derived from them. The place to present those earlier findings and conclusions is in the review of literature. Thus we must write this chapter with some anticipation of what we might need in later chapters. This often means that just as we re-read an introduction after finishing the results chapter, so we may wish to add to the review of the literature when we write the discussion and conclusions' (Fox, 1969, p 726–7).

- we should cover all points of view in the field, including those which differ from or are opposite to the author's. To achieve this it is useful to make a careful distinction between summaries of the thinking of others and critical analysis of that thinking.

❏ Bibliography

Bell, J. (1987) *Doing Your Research Project A Guide for First-Time Researchers in Education and Social Science*, Milton Keynes: Open University Press

Bell, J. and Goulding, S. (1984) 'Sources, records and references: a guide for students planning investigations in educational management', in Bell, J. et al. (Eds) *Conducting Small-Scale Investigations in Educational Management*, London: Harper and Row

Fox, D.J. (1969) *The Research Process in Education*, New York: Holt, Reinhart and Winston

Haywood, P. and Wragg, E.C. (1982) *Evaluating the Literature*, Rediguide 2, Nottingham University School of Education

Merriam, S.B. (1988) *Case Study Research in Education A Qualitative Approach*, San Francisco: Jossey-Bass

University of Leicester MBA in educational management by distance learning

The MBA in educational management by distance learning is a unique qualification which combines an academically rigorous programme with personal development in the context of institutional improvement. The degree is a *partnership* between the teacher, their school or college and the University.

The course balances knowledge with reflection leading to application; this is achieved through:

- *High quality, relevant and up-to-date course materials*
- *Resources designed to help understanding and personal reflection*
- *Assessment linked to practical management outcomes*

The degree is academically and professionally demanding but will form the basis for enhanced management effectiveness, career development and personal growth.

The degree can be made up of a combination of distance learning materials, school- or college-based activity and, in appropriate circumstances, the accreditation of prior learning.

The MBA is a genuinely distance learning qualification. This means that you decide:

- *when you start to study*
- *the pace at which you study*
- *the specialist focus of your degree*
- *the topics for assessment*
- *where and when you study*

There are no compulsory residentials or formal tutorials. Advice and support are available through:

- *Telephone and fax advice lines*
- *A regional network of tutors*
- *High quality course materials*
- *Study groups*
- *Linking with school/college based activities*
- *Networking with other course members*

Further information is available in the course handbook. This information is subject to confirmation by the University of Leicester Senate.

Course structure

The degree programme is made up of a planning unit and five modules:

1. Leadership and strategic management

2. Managing the curriculum

3. The management of professional and support staff

4. Managing finance and external relations

5. Research methods

The planning unit is designed to help you plan your programme of study and the most effective ways of integrating the degree into your work, professional and career development.

Each module is made up of a core unit which is compulsory, an elective unit chosen from a range of options and a 5,000 word assignment. Module 5 is a compulsory course in research methods followed by a 20,000 word project on a management subject.

	Planning Unit		
Module			
1	Core	Elective	⟶ Assignment
2	Core	Elective	⟶ Assignment
3	Core	Elective	⟶ Assignment
4	Core	Elective	⟶ Assignment
5	Core		⟶ Management Project

❑ Examples of elective units

Total Quality Management; Relationships with the Governing Body; The Curriculum and Learning in the Secondary School; Women in Educational Management; Management of Teams in the Special School; Managing Staff Development in the Primary School and Quality Assurance in Further Education.

Course materials

When you have been accepted on to the course you will receive a copy of *The Principles of Educational Management*. This is the core text which will serve as an introduction to the advanced study of education management and be a major reference work throughout the course.

When you register for a particular unit you will receive a learning pack which will include:

— an authoritative discussion of the topic

— activities, exercises and readings

— application to real cases in schools and colleges

— coverage of current issues

— suggestions for further study and reading

Awards

1 Module	=	Advanced Certificate in Educational Management
4 Modules	=	Postgraduate Diploma in Educational Management
5 Modules	=	MBA in Educational Management

For further information please contact: Carolyn Vincent, Course Manager, University Centre, Queens Building, Barrack Road, Northampton, NN2 6AF. Tel: 0604 30180

University of Leicester
Educational Management Development Unit

The Educational Management Development Unit (EMDU) is a specialist unit within the University of Leicester School of Education. It was established in January 1992 with the specific brief to offer high quality training and development programmes to meet the management needs of professionals working in schools and colleges.

The EMDU offers:

- Accredited courses leading to Higher level qualifications
- School-based development activities
- Consultancy
- Distance learning packages

EMDU aims to build on the recommendations of the School Development Task Force and offers management training to meet the needs of senior managers and those aspiring to such positions. It offers qualifications geared to the management needs of schools and colleges in the 1990s.

EMDU aims to meet the needs of individuals and institutions. The MBA in Educational Management is offered in part-time and distance learning modes.

It covers all aspects of educational management and is designed for people holding or aspiring to senior management positions in schools and colleges.

The Advanced Certificate (school-based) in Educational Management is an exciting new opportunity for schools to negotiate a tailor-made programme, designed to meet the school's needs, at a much lower cost than conventional University taught modules.

EMDU offers consultancy and associated training/development activities to schools and colleges on an individual basis. EMDU staff provide advice and expertise in all aspects of educational management.

EMDU is engaged in a range of research activities — current topics include:

— Quality management in education

— Self-governing schools

— Middle management

— Theories of educational management

— Women in educational management

— Mentoring and school management

— Managing the curriculum

EMDU works with individuals, individual schools and colleges, and also with groups of teachers or institutions. EMDU aims to help education professionals determine training and development needs and then sets out to provide high quality training packages designed to meet those needs. EMDU aims to provide development packages which can be combined to lead to a variety of qualifications in Educational Management.

The Centre for Total Quality in Education and the Community is based in EMDU. This is the first centre to be specifically dedicated to research and development into Total Quality in schools and colleges.

For further information about the work of EMDU please contact: Professor Tony Bush, EMDU, School of Education, Queens Building, Barrack Road, Northampton, NN2 6AF

Author index

Index